HISTORY OF
THE UNITED STATES

THE RECORD OF 1970-71

THE MARCH
OF DEMOCRACY

A HISTORY OF THE UNITED STATES

By James Truslow Adams

Continued by Gaetano L. Vincitorio

Professor of History, St. John's University, New York

THE RECORD OF 1970-71

CHARLES SCRIBNER'S SONS
NEW YORK

1 3 5 7 9 11 13 15 17 19 C/C 20 18 16 14 12 10 8 6 4 2

PRINTED IN THE UNITED STATES OF AMERICA
LIBRARY OF CONGRESS CATALOG CARD·NUMBER 38–34425
ISBN 0–684–13733–X

ILLUSTRATIONS

THE RECORD OF 1970–1971

T HIS ISSUE OF the *Record* covers the events of two years, rather than the customary one. And since 1970 and 1971 were more than ordinarily filled with incident and controversy, the usual narrative form has been abandoned in favor of a topical treatment. It is hoped that this approach and method will aid clarity and coherence.

The order of the topics, each of which occupies a separate chapter, is as follows: 1. A brief introduction on the general state of the nation; 2. The President; 3. The Congress; 4. The War in Southeast Asia; 5. Foreign Policy; 6. The National Economy; 7. The Judiciary; 8. Civil Rights and Minorities; 9. Education and Youth Problems; 10. The Women's Liberation Protest; 11. Space Exploration and Transportation; 12. General comments.

THE STATE OF THE NATION

The feeling so pervasive in some quarters during the late 1960's that the American soul was in turmoil carried over into the next decade. In the view of some Marxists and radicals, Americans were experiencing the "contradictions of capitalism;" therefore, if healing were to be had, Americans would have to scrap the whole structure of

7

corporate and private ownership and control and establish a completely new social system. Various thoughtful (and less doctrinaire) observers saw the causes and the cure of the malady in different lights. Andrew Hacker, the political scientist, did not lay the blame on wrongheaded policies or inept politicians but on the fact that Americans have become too self-centered—that they prefer their comforts and personal pleasures to collective endeavors necessary for the welfare of society. Daniel Boorstin, the distinguished historian, contended that many Americans were too concerned with the needs of the moment; that they were therefore morbidly preoccupied with themselves and either magnified or imagined a host of national ills. Lacking a sense of history, and consequently unable to compare present conditions against the achievement of their own ancestors or against those of other peoples in the past, Americans rashly conclude that theirs is the worst of all societies and this is the worst of all times. Boorstin added that their obsession with speed has bred in them a colossal impatience with efforts to improve conditions.

The mood of many Americans was more optimistic than a year before, but it was still far from sanguine. They saw the end of the long Vietnamese war in sight and they were confident that solutions for the pressing economic problems were not far off. There was a noticeable tendency on the part of some leaders and the public at large to end the hypercritical self-evaluation of American life. Stickers on car bumpers read, "America, Love It or Leave It." Decals of the flag were proudly displayed on windshields, in business offices, and on work clothing. President Nixon gave voice to largely inarticulate sentiment when he told the cheering members of the Junior Chamber of Commerce ("Jaycees") at St. Louis in June 1970 that, "It is time to stand up and speak out about what is right about America . . . America is a good country and we are going to make her better."

The optimism was rendered less enthusiastic by many old irritants. Americans resented what they labelled the "welfare mess." They believed that too many able-bodied persons were living well at their expense while the government continued to bleed hard-working citizens to support the idle. They were deeply worried over street crime (the crime rate in 1970 was eleven percent higher than the year before) and the apparent failure of the authorities, especially the courts, to do anything about it. Their anger at enforced school busing by the courts and by persistent unemployment was high. Other old worries, the welfare of their children, the growing addiction to drugs, the pollution of water and air, weighed heavily on them. Most black people felt that the country generally, and the Nixon Administration in particular, were not responsive to their needs and to their aspirations.

Not least among the irritants were criminal civil disturbances. The Capitol building itself was not immune from bombing. On March 1, 1971 a device exploded in a wing. An anonymous telephone call announced that the bombing was in protest against the United States presence in Laos. Street riots, explosion of bombs in Reserve Officers' Training Corps buildings and in other government facilities, and shootings of policemen were sources of concern in 1970 and 1971. So were the avowed intentions of radical groups. The Weatherman faction of Students for a Democratic Society which had engaged in the revolutionary "days of rage" in Chicago in October 1969, the Black Panthers whose slogan was "Kill the Pigs" (law enforcement officers), the Student National Coordinating Committee (SNCC), and the Black Liberation Army were only the more prominent of the groups advocating and employing violence to achieve their goals.

Yet the Federal government could really do little about the type of crime that worried Americans most—street crimes: holdups and muggings, murders, rapes, robberies, burglaries, and auto thefts. Some cities did record a decline in overall crime but were unable to reduce the incidents to acceptable levels.

An additional source of anxiety was the computerization of information by credit bureaus and other business agencies. Even more alarming was government "snooping," or the process of gathering and storing in a computer bank detailed personal information on millions of Americans drawn from the files of the Social Security Administration, the Internal Revenue Service, the Veterans Administration, HEW, and other agencies. The chairman of the Senate Subcommittee on Constitutional Rights, Sam J. Ervin, Jr., of North Carolina, lamented the possibility that "instant blacklisting, ready cross-country exchange of dossiers, million-name master indexes, and scientific surveillance can easily become the order of the political day"—all made possible by the modern computer. The threat to privacy caused some to believe that the tyranny of "big brother" described by George

Orwell in his novel *1984* might come to pass in their lifetime.

Some libertarians feared that the spying was even extended to members of Congress; and they abhorred the collection of data by the Secret Service on about 50,000 activists, malcontents, and questionable persons. Their complaints centered on J. Edgar Hoover, for over 45 years the Director of the FBI. The House Majority Leader, Hale Boggs of Louisiana, accused Hoover of tapping the telephones of members of Congress, a charge denied by Hoover and the Attorney-General. Hoover was also attacked for telling a Senate subcommittee that there was an alleged plot to kidnap Henry A. Kissinger, the presidential adviser, in which the Reverend Philip Berrigan, a Catholic radical, and other antiwar activists were involved. But the demand voiced by some for Hoover's resignation received little general support. On March 8, 1971, nearly 800 secret documents were removed from the FBI office in Media, Pennsylvania, by the so-called "Citizens' Commission to Investigate the FBI" which sent copies of reports on radical blacks and campus groups to the press and others.

The open attacks on the public and private morality cherished by Americans since colonial days were especially disturbing. "Sexploitation" movies made the "stag" movies of a generation ago seem pallid by comparison. Even films designed for general audiences, rated "GP" by the movie industry (that is General Patronage, Parental Guidance Suggested), dealt with themes once reserved for discussion by abnormal psychologists or they glorified the "antihero" who had no moral convictions.

Homosexual activists judged the times propitious to press for "gay rights" and the repeal of legislation forbidding sexual practices universally condemned for thousands of years. Some even demanded the right to "marry" and found a few ministers of religion who obliged them.

Many Americans demanded government action on these matters and were displeased at the report of the Federal Commission on Obscenity which recommended the dropping of all legal barriers to "the sale, exhibition, or distribution of sexual materials to consenting adults." It denied that pornography played an important part in causing crime, delinquency, sexual aberration, or emotional disturbance. Some members of the panel urged that legal restrictions be lifted on sexual materials for children as well. A minority of the Commission charged that pornography threatened America with moral bankruptcy and that the report was a "magna charta for the pornographer."

Organizations like Citizens for Decent Literature damned the Commission for compounding the problems of America and leading the nation to ruin. President Nixon characterized the majority report as morally bankrupt.

The main obstacle to cleaning up pornography, in the view of many, was the Supreme Court. Meanwhile, in response to complaints that pornographic materials were being sent through the mails and often to children, Congress tacked on to the postal reorganization bill a provision authorizing persons who did not wish to receive sex-oriented advertising to signify their wish to the postal service.

Two developments in the last decade continued to disturb thoughtful observers. The first was the general public expectation of more democratic social change and of additional creature comforts; the second was civil disobedience. Since the days of the New Deal, the Federal government had helped to generate the rising expectations of the American people and employed its vast powers and the resources of the nation to fulfill them. Rarely before in history did so many come to expect so much of their country and its government in their quest for the "good life," which was commonly regarded as a peaceful life filled with ease and comfort. Perhaps such expectations are really beyond reach.

The unfulfilled expectations in turn cast suspicion on the legitimacy of the "establishment" forces in their efforts to meet the violence accompanying change. Frequently, political and other leaders made the task of maintaining respect for law even more difficult by seeking to avert further trouble on the part of the poor, the blacks, and the young by condoning some of the violence and buying off the militants by big concessions. Since this implied that violence or the threat of force "paid off," some reformers and unionists were led to assume that the basic social and political changes which they wanted were indeed to be had by threatening to break the peace. Of course, the emphasis on force caused a reaction on the part of other Americans in favor of "law and order" and the local police, who were always the first to bear the brunt of the resentment of disappointed reformers and militants. On July 4, 1970, a large rally took place in Washington, D.C. for "Honor America Day."

13

The other development of the 1960's which carried over to the 1970's—civil disobedience—was an element in the numerous protests against the war in Vietnam or against features of American life that some young people and reformers wanted to change. It is defined as the public and peaceful refusal to obey governmental authority for the sake of moral principle. It aims at persuading the people by symbolic acts (the burning of draft cards or records, or the refusal to pay taxes) and by defiance of the laws only to agitate for certain changes within the existing legal and political system.

Opponents of civil disobedience said that such a doctrine was inimical to public order because it made obedience voluntary; it deprived the law of its binding power by granting the right to disobey to anybody whose conscience directed him to oppose the law. They also asserted that the fine line between "peaceful" and violent acts disappears in practice during boycotts, strikes, and demonstrations. Bashed skulls, street riots, and property damage were common results of peaceful protest, they concluded. The great danger posed by civil disobedience lay in prospects of total breakdown when major groups, and not minorities, would decide to employ the successful tactics of disruption and refusal to obey.

THE PRESIDENT

Richard M. Nixon gained confidence and force after his first year in office. A solitary figure, isolated from the ordinary contacts of politicians and office holders by his chief of staff, H. R. Haldeman, he pushed vigorously ahead toward his main goals of disengaging American forces in Southeast Asia, adopting a more flexible position toward the hostile Communist world, hurling defiance at domestic militants, and solving the vexing economic problems. He spent some working vacations at the western White House in San Clemente, California, at Camp David in the Maryland mountains, and in his home at Key Biscayne, Florida. The American people in general were well disposed toward the President, his gracious First Lady, and his daughters. Widespread interest followed the marriage of Tricia, his eldest daughter, to Edward Finch Cox in the Rose Garden of the White House on June 12, 1971.

He met with difficulty—expectedly, from the liberal press and, unexpectedly, from conservatives. He saw the press less often than recent Presidents, and his relations with the press and television were far from cordial. The Nixon Administration through Vice President Agnew charged that the news media were neither fair nor impartial in reporting and interpreting national events; that in the guise of furnishing information the press and television newscasters were actually engaged in political and social controversy; and that when criticized they placed themselves under the protection of the First Amendment. Agnew's was merely the most prominent of many voices in and out of politics who regretted the transformation of journalists into advocates for peace, social reform, civil rights, or other causes, and the resulting blurring of the distinction between news reports and editorial opinion.

Newspapers were reverting, according to this view, to what they had been in the early years of the Republic, agents for party.

Miss Edith Efron in *The News Twisters* presented statistical evidence that the major networks (ABC, CBS, and NBC) were hostile to Richard Nixon, to the American role in Vietnam, and had a distinct liberal bias; that they portrayed the Left as "harmless, friendly, idealistic, funny, young, 'restless', and trustworthy." In short that the networks were guilty of misrepresentation.

Nixon's position with the American Right weakened. For years he had traded on his vigorous anti-Communism, but after he became President, the opinion grew that he was no conservative; that he took no really effective measures against big government or Communism or for constitutional, limited government, national vital interests, and American patriotism. Instead, he favored unbalanced budgets and accommodation with the giants of the Communist world. What galvanized conservative opposition was his announcement that he would visit Peking, the capital of Red China.

They grumbled over his own characterization of himself in an exclusive interview that he gave to the *New York Times,* the citadel of eastern liberalism. He said that he was a devoted pacifist. His critics charged that he was ready to sacrifice American security for a promise of good behavior by Russia, Red China, and other aggressive powers. James J. Kilpatrick asked "What Happened to Our Skipper," and noted the dilemma of conservatives. "We are not ready to abandon ship: Where do we swim to? . . . The rueful notion will not go away that we preferred our skipper then [1968] to our skipper now." Some conservatives were shaken by what they regarded as a policy of defeat-and-retreat in Vietnam rather than the "honorable peace" the President said that he was searching for in his eight-point offer to Hanoi. As James Burnham wrote, "Henry Kissinger in Paris was negotiating not victory or peace but surrender."

The President's conduct of government relied more on White House advisers like H. R. Haldeman and John Ehrlichman and relatively less on members of his Cabinet. In June, 1970, Mr. Nixon named Elliot L. Richardson to head HEW, replacing Robert H. Finch who became counselor to the President. James D. Hodgson became Secretary of Labor in place of George P. Schultz, who became director of the Office of Management and Budget. The most controversial member of the Cabinet was Walter J. Hickel of Alaska, the Secretary of the Interior, who did not maintain good relations with his chief. In a letter to the President of May 6, 1970 (leaked to the press before Mr. Nixon read it), Hickel criticized him for alienating young people and for isolating himself from his Cabinet. The Secretary had been most critical of the administration's policy in Southeast Asia. Citing lack of mutual confidence, the President replaced Hickel with Rogers C. B. Morton of Kentucky, the Republican National Chairman. Another Cabinet change was the appointment of John B. Connally, a Democrat and former Governor of Texas, in place of David M. Kennedy as Secretary of the Treasury. Connally assumed a position of leadership and importance not only in economic affairs but in all phases of government.

The size of the Cabinet was reduced to eleven when the new U.S. Postal Service became operative on July 1, 1971, in accordance with the Postal Reorganization Act of 1970, which provided for a government-owned corporation with the power to appoint postmasters and to set postal rates and pay. The way had been prepared for the new system by a strike of postal workers that led to the declaration of a state of emergency in March 1970 and the ordering of Federal troops into New York City to move the mails.

Mr. Nixon urged the reorganization of the Cabinet in 1971. His plan called for eight posts: State, Defense, Justice, and Treasury would remain. Four new ones, namely, Natural Resources, Human Resources, Economic Development, and Community Development would encompass the other seven existing departments. Congressmen, officials, farmers, and businessmen criticized the proposals. The President bowed to pressure and agreed to keep Agriculture separate in the reorganization plan. His nomination of Earl L. Butz to replace Clifford M. Hardin as Secretary of Agriculture touched off opposition from farm groups which insisted that Butz favored large-scale or corporate farming. The Senate confirmed his appointment after a sharp debate, 51–44.

THE CONGRESS

1.

When the 91st Congress met in January 1970, the questions dividing it and the nation concerned Indochina, the unrest of the young, growing violence, inflation and unemployment, and of course the forthcoming elections in November.

The Senate had 57 Democrats, 43 Republicans; the House had 245 Democrats, 188 Republicans, and 2 vacancies. The Majority Leader in the Senate remained Mike J. Mansfield of Montana, and the Democratic Whip, Edward M. Kennedy of Massachusetts. Their Republican counterparts were Hugh D. Scott, Jr., of Pennsylvania, and Robert P. Griffin of Michigan. In the House, John W. McCormack of Massachusetts was Speaker and Carl B. Albert of Oklahoma, the Majority Leader; Gerald R. Ford of Michigan was Minority Leader, and Leslie C. Arends of Illinois, the Minority Whip. The first Congressional reform in almost a quarter century was enacted in the Legislative Reorganization Act of 1970. In the House, all votes in committee were to be made public. Teller votes were to be recorded by name of the congressman as was the case in roll-call votes, and not in the total number of those voting as hitherto had been the practice. The Act also permitted broadcasting and televising of House committee hearings; it streamlined operations and provided for improved research and information.

In his first State of the Union message (January 22, 1970), President Nixon promised to turn his attention to curtailing the mounting internal problems of water and environmental pollution, to pressing the war on crime and on inflation, to reforming the social welfare system, and to sponsoring revenue-sharing with States and with local authorities. Alluding to the great expectations that Americans had come to have in the ability of government to provide the good life for all, he said that "As a people we had too many visions and too little vision." He maintained that America could abolish hunger, provide means for every family to get a minimum income, better housing, faster transportation, improved health, and superior education.

The first big legislative battle between the Congress and the President was over spending. When Congress added to a health, education, and antipoverty appropriations bill, Mr. Nixon vetoed the measure in January 1970 because it was inflationary. The House failed to override the veto. A compromise appropriations bill for approximately $17.4 billion was finally hammered out after seven months of disagreement. In June, Congress overrode the veto of a hospital construction and modernization authorization bill which the President considered fiscally irresponsible. In August, it also overrode his veto of appropriations of $4.4 billion for the Office of Education, but did sustain his veto of an $18.1 billion appropriations for various other agencies.

In his State of the Union message in January 1970 the President had asked: "Shall we surrender to our surroundings or shall we make our peace with nature and begin to make reparations for the damage we have done to our air, to our land and to our water?" Reforms in the matter of the environment were not only expedient politically, but necessary. In February he issued an order to Federal agencies to eliminate all air and water pollution which they caused. Concern was expressed over such matters as the disposal of solid wastes, and smoke and fumes that polluted water and air. Young people were especially active in efforts to arouse Americans to the urgency of the problem. They held a nationwide "teach-in" on Earth Day, April 22, 1970. Although he approved of the observance, Mr. Nixon did not explicitly participate in it. To implement the National Environmental Policy Act, the President appointed a Council on Environmental Quality. By the end of the year Congress passed the Clean Air Act which required auto manufacturers to make autos 90 percent pollution-free by 1975.

The President sought international cooperation to end pollution since it was a problem common to all highly industrialized countries. The International Joint Committee recommended to the American and Canadian Governments in 1971 that they take appropriate steps to control pollution in the Great Lakes and the St. Lawrence River. It recommended that the phosphate level in laundry detergents be limited and eventually eliminated, and that there be undertaken a program of removing phosphates in treating wastes. At a conference, the United States and Canada agreed on a joint program to clean up the waters of the Great Lakes by 1975 and to establish common water-quality standards.

In 1970 Congress passed the District of Columbia Crime Bill which was designed to be a model for other cities. It permitted police in possession of a search or arrest warrant to enter the house of a suspect without announcing their arrival ("no knock"), and judges to hold suspects for 60 days in "preventive detention" if those persons posed a danger to the community.

The Department of Justice continued to fund the improvement of local police forces, courts, and prison systems through the Law Enforcement Assistance Administration. It also utilized the strike-force concept against organized crime; thereby bringing together a team drawn from the Bureau of Narcotic and Dangerous Drugs, the FBI, the Internal Revenue Service, and other Federal enforcement agencies under the direction of an attorney from the Department of Justice to wage a unified assault against entrenched wrongdoers in a certain "target area" of particular cities and metropolitan areas. In 1971 some 600 Federal indictments were made of organized crime figures.

Drugs were a special source of concern. The widespread use of marijuana or "pot" was highlighted by the arrest of children of prominent Americans, including sons of the late Robert Kennedy, of R. Sargent Shriver III, and of Governor William T. Cahill of New Jersey. Death from overdoses of hard drugs touched well-known figures in the youth world. Singer-guitarist Jimi Hendrix and blues queen Janis Joplin were victims. A House committee said in 1971 that 50 to 60 percent of American servicemen in Vietnam had at least experimented with marijuana, and that as many as 10 to 15 percent used heroin or other hard drugs. The problem in Vietnam was compounded by the involvement in the drug traffic of corrupt officials in South Vietnam, Laos, or Thailand.

It was one thing to lament the drug problem; it was quite another to find a solution. Most Americans wanted strict enforcement of existing laws banning the use of marijuana and heroin; but some others recommended that penalties for the use of marijuana either be softened or eliminated altogether. A howl of criticism greeted the recommendations of the Commission on Reform of Federal Criminal Laws headed by former Governor of California, Edmund G. Brown. After a four-year study, the Commission urged that the possession of marijuana be punished by fine, not imprisonment; that the death penalty be abolished for Federal crimes; and that the manufacture sale, and possession of handguns—except for law enforcement officers—be banned.

The Comprehensive Drug Abuse Prevention and Control Act of 1970 provided severe penalties for drug pushers and peddlers, but the problem seemed to grow worse. In June 1970, Mr. Nixon sent a message to Congress on drug abuse which he characterized as a national emergency. He announced the creation of a Special Action Office of Drug Abuse Prevention. His belief was that "If we cannot destroy the drug menace in America, then it will surely in time destroy us." He asked Congress for more money to rehabilitate drug users, to strengthen enforcement, and to halt the drug traffic by illicit producers of drugs. In view of the fact that the sources for heroin were outside the country, the Nixon Administration undertook to reach agreements with a number of foreign countries (France and Mexico, for example) to cooperate with American efforts to curtail the drug traffic.

In response to the public outrage at violence and crime, Congress passed the Organized Crime Control Act which established Federal control over explosives in interstate commerce; provided for the death penalty for persons convicted of a fatal bombing; empowered the Federal government to prosecute persons accused of arson and bombing on college campuses; made it a crime to use money from organized crime to start a business engaged in interstate trade; and authorized judges to impose an additional sentence of twenty-five years on "dangerous and adult special offenders."

New housing was needed in many parts of the land, but competing demands of a need for housing and the need to curb inflation led the President to veto in August 1970 an appropriations bill that provided over $3.5 billion for the purpose. Nevertheless, house construction under Federal subsidy programs increased. In July 1970, the President had signed the Emergency Housing Act. This was designed to produce 1.3 million new housing units by providing interest subsidies to Savings and Loan associations and more mortgage funds to the Government National Mortgage Association. In December 1970, Congress authorized over $2.8 billion for housing and related projects, including Federal crime-insurance covering burglary, theft, robbery, and larceny in cases where ordinary insurance could not be secured; also for permitting the Community Development Corporation to lend money to new community developers in HUD-approved programs.

The effort of HUD under George Romney to encourage low-cost housing by introducing new technology into housing construction was only partially successful. Many suburban communities resisted low-cost housing that would bring in blacks and other minorities. They received the support of the President when he said that forced integration in the suburbs was not in the national interest.

A significant Congressional action was the lowering of the voting age to eighteen. Congress passed a bill reducing the voting age in Federal, State, and local elections from 21 to 18 years. This was signed by Mr. Nixon in June 1970, but not before noting that there were doubts about its constitutionality and directing the Attorney-General to expedite a court test of the measure. The bill also extended until 1975 the Voting Rights Act of 1965; prohibited literacy tests to be employed as qualifications for voting; provided for a uniform thirty-day residence requirement for voting in presidential elections; and extended the Act to parts of six states (parts of New York City, districts in Alaska, Arizona, etc.) where less than half the people of voting age had registered or voted in the 1968 Presidential election.

The Nixon Administration anticipated that the mid-term elections of 1970 would give the Republicans a larger number of Representatives and the control of the Senate, and so enable it to carry out its programs in Congress.

The President took an active role in the November elections. Stumping over twenty states, he denounced the wave of violence and terrorism by radical antidemocratic elements and he urged the end of appeasing "thugs and hoodlums." Vice President Agnew also traveled widely and blasted "radical-liberals" who opposed Mr. Nixon in the Senate. The appeal of the Republicans was to "law and order," while the Democratic slogan was raised against inflation and unemployment.

The electorate did not record a clear-cut decision on these issues. In Philadelphia, Frank L. Rizzo, a Democrat but a supporter of Mr. Nixon, defeated a liberal Republican for mayor of that city; but Representative Louise Day Hicks, who had a national reputation for "law and order" and opposition to school busing, lost in her bid to become mayor of Boston. The Republicans made a net gain of one Senate seat (plus another who would vote with them), while the Democrats added nine seats in the House and wrested eleven governorships from their rivals. Two Nixon foes lost in the Senate: Charles Goodell (Republican of New York) and Albert Gore (Democrat of Tennessee). A surprise victor in a three-way race in New York was James L. Buckley, a Conservative, who ousted the incumbent Goodell. The lineup of 32 Republican and 18 Democratic governors was changed to 29 Democrats and 21 Republicans.

The 92nd Congress, therefore, would have 54 Democrats, 45 Republicans, and one vacancy in the Senate; 254 Democrats and 180 Republicans in the House and one vacancy. Mike Mansfield was again chosen Majority Leader by the Senate Democrats, but Senator Robert C. Byrd of West Virginia was made Majority Whip in place of Senator Edward M. Kennedy. The new Speaker of the House was Carl B. Albert of Oklahoma and Hale Boggs of Louisiana became Majority Leader. There was no change for the Republicans.

2.

In January 1971 the President presented the 92nd Congress with his "Six Great Goals." These were (1) reform of the welfare system, (2) full prosperity in peacetime, (3) restore and enhance the natural environment, (4) im-

26

prove health and medical care, (5) strengthen and renew State and local governments by revenue-sharing with States and localities, (6) reform of the Executive branch of government.

Congress took a partisan view of the President's proposals, regarding them as intended for public consumption in preparation for the campaign in 1972. Measures proposed or supported by Mr. Nixon were stalled in committee. And wherever the Democratic majority favored a presidential idea, they substituted their own specific proposals to achieve the goal in question. When the 1971 fiscal year ended on June 30, only three out of fourteen required appropriation bills for the next year were passed, so that some government departments had to operate without appropriated funds. The President and the Congress hurled mutual charges about the responsibility for the delay in the necessary legislation. It is possible that public confidence in the system of divided responsibility between the Executive and the Legislative branches was shaken.

As in previous years, the President was ascendant in foreign policy (save for disputes over Vietnam) but he had to fight for each inch of the way on the road to achieving his domestic policy. In his contest with the 92nd Congress in its first session in 1971, Mr. Nixon got only part of his proposals accepted. Yet his victories were impressive: a tax-relief program; power to control wages and prices in Phase Two of his economic plan; confirmation of Justices Powell and Rehnquist to the Supreme Court and of Earl Butz as Secretary of Agriculture. Congress acceded to his wishes in rejecting a fixed date for withdrawing all U.S. forces to Vietnam, in sustaining his veto of the Democratic-sponsored multibillion-dollar day-care center program, and also of a bill providing public service jobs for the unemployed.

Congress, however, rejected the continued development of the supersonic transport plane (SST) begun in 1963 by President Kennedy. In May 1971, Congress refused to appropriate further funds for continuing the project which had been so costly to the government and the airlines. Arguments against the SST centered on its high cost and possible damage to the environment. The rejection left the field of large supersonic transports to the Anglo-French *Concorde* and the Russian TU-144.

And Congress dogged the President on defense-related funds. After acrimonious debate in the summer of 1971, Congress permitted the government to guarantee up to $250 million worth of bank loans to an American company whose possible bankruptcy would have seriously and adversely affected the economy. This measure was aimed at saving the Lockheed Aircraft Corporation of California, the country's largest defense contractor, which was producing 400 passenger jets—the L-1011 TriStar, whose engines were being manufactured by Rolls-Royce of Great Britain. In the process of supplying the engines to Lockheed, Rolls-Royce went bankrupt. Negotiations between the American and British governments led to an agreement whereby Washington guaranteed the TriStar project. The debate in Congress raised questions over using taxpayer money to support allegedly free enterprise.

The 92nd Congress showed its independence in refusing assent to proposals of the President relating to revenue-sharing, reorganizing the Federal government, and overhauling the welfare system.

In 1971 the President announced a series of proposals to render more responsive and efficient the relationship between the Federal government and the States, localities, and individuals. He proposed a $16 billion program of general and special revenue sharing with States and localities. General sharing referred to Federal revenues that would be turned over directly to the States and localities to be spent as the recipients saw fit. Special revenue sharing funds would go to State and local authorities for manpower, law enforcement, education, transportation, urban, and rural development. Mr. Nixon's plan was tied up in committee. There was general agreement that the States had to be strengthened if the Federal system of government were to be effective. Since the States were a microcosm of the nation, they were beset with similar problems of economy, pollution, youth, drugs, and crime which required vast outlays of money which they found difficult to raise. The expenditures of cities for schools, police and other services, and welfare soared while their tax base shrank as corporations relocated in the suburbs and middle-class whites escaped the crime and congestion of urban areas. The white city dwellers were replaced by poorer blacks and other minorities like Puerto Ricans and Mexican-Americans (Chicanos) who required an expansion of municipal services. This situation was dramatized by some New Yorkers who wanted to make their city the 51st State. Whether or not this was a mere tactic in the old struggle for money between city politicians and State legislators and governors is difficult to assess.

The concern with urban problems obsessed some politicians and reformers who saw racial tensions, poor housing in ghettoes, urban congestion, corrupt or inefficient city government, and the breakdowns in private and public transportation as calling for immediate and drastic Federal action. Republican national leaders were not overly sympathetic to the pleas of persons who spoke of urban crisis and who were, more often than not, their partisan opponents. Professor Edward C. Banfield of Harvard University opposed the view of the overwhelming majority of political scientists when he said in his book, *The Unheavenly City,* that the cries to meet the urban crisis served the selfish purposes of politicians, civil rights leaders, bureaucrats, and guilt-ridden do-gooders, and that nothing or little can be done about the cities. The latter would really profit from "benign neglect."

Congress and the President heard many complaints about the "welfare mess." Many States took measures to hold down the costs of welfare, insisting that able-bodied recipients register at State employment offices, and that financially-able relatives help to support them. The number of Americans on welfare in 1971 was 14.3 million; and the cost $16.2 billion. Despite the public clamor the Department of Health, Education, and Welfare maintained that many complaints were exaggerated: that welfare recipients were not living "high on the hog"; that they spent their money largely on necessities; that the vast majority was honest; and that less than one percent were able-bodied men.

The Nixon Administration submitted a proposal for overhauling existing State and local welfare programs which were a patchwork of over eleven hundred separate units. It recommended a guaranteed minimum annual income of $1600 for a family of four, which could earn more by working so that its total could reach $3920. It might also utilize food-stamp allotments for participating in work-training programs. Although the House accepted the Nixon proposals, the Senate Finance Committee did not. Late in 1971, Congress did act to secure limited welfare reform by establishing work requirements for welfare recipients, requiring able-bodied adult recipients—except the aged and mothers of children under 6—to register for job training.

In March 1971, a law increased Social Security benefits by ten percent. The increases necessitated hikes in the payroll tax (up to 6.05 percent by 1987) and in the amount of wages subject to taxes (increased to $9000 in 1972).

The 92nd Congress amended a tax bill allowing any citizen after 1973 to earmark one dollar of his tax payments for a political contribution. This was regarded by Republicans as a partisan measure aimed at swelling the coffers of the debt-ridden Democrats who had a larger popular enrollment.

The inherent difficulty of Mr. Nixon's relation with Congress lay in the fact that he was Republican and both Houses were in Democratic hands. He was the first President in over a century to take office without the control of Congress by his own party. In 1970–1971 the working relationship between the Executive and Legislative branches was good but not intimate. The Senate Democratic Leader Mike Mansfield rated the President's performance as extremely good in foreign relations and "over all he hasn't done too badly" in domestic matters. No doubt, part of his difficulty was his lack of success in fostering good congressional relations by consulting congressmen and being sensitive to their patronage needs.

What was happening in Congress was a straining of the two-party system. A voting alliance of Republicans and Southern Democrats against Northern Democrats appeared in 1971 in 30 percent of all recorded votes and prevailed in 80 percent of the votes in which it appeared. The President's dominance over Congress despite many setbacks was impressive. It was estimated that he won over 90 percent of his public stands, pro and con. It should be noted that there was growing evidence not only of a conservative coalition but of modern-Republican, liberal-Democratic cooperation as well.

The absenteeism during roll calls of many liberal Senators, especially potential Democratic presidential candidates, hurt the liberal cause. Senator George McGovern for example, voted in 50 percent of the roll calls in which the conservative coalition appeared.

THE WAR IN SOUTHEAST ASIA

I.

The nation's main preoccupation in 1970–1971 continued to be the war in Southeast Asia. President Nixon announced on December 15, 1969, that another 50,000 troops would be pulled out of Vietnam within four months because the peace talks in Paris were progressing well, the training of South Vietnamese forces was succeeding, and the level of enemy activity had diminished. He continued to reject any suggestion that the United States withdraw unilaterally. "Precipitate withdrawal," he said, would have tragic consequences. In October 1970, he proposed a cease-fire in Indochina supervised by international observers, the withdrawal of American forces under certain conditions, and the convening of a peace conference. His policy toward Indochina included negotiation with the enemy and "Vietnamization." In order to speed up the process of negotiation, he halted the bombing of North Vietnam, agreed to accept the Vietcong (National Liberation Front) as a party to the negotiations, and to withdraw more U.S. forces. Vietnamization aimed at strengthening the armed forces of South Vietnam so that they could defend the country, and extending the pacification program—that is, interdicting support and supplies for the Vietcong from the countryside and thereby affirming control of the rural areas by the government in Saigon.

In 1968 and 1969 the Allied forces had managed to limit severely the ability of the North Vietnamese to supply their troops in the South. Supplies were brought down the Ho Chi Minh Trail—from North Vietnam down through the Plain of Jarres in eastern Laos into Cambodia, and finally to South Vietnam. Early in 1970, the North Vietnamese joined the pro-Communist guerrillas in Laos in attacking the government. The Laotian forces, however, managed to cut the trail in places and thereby jeopardize the flow of Communist supplies to the south.

Congressional leaders objected to the widening of the

Indochina war by a growing participation of American advisers and airmen in Laos. Senator William Fulbright (Democrat of Arkansas), the chairman of the Foreign Relations Committee, introduced a resolution (March 1970) that prevented the extension of the war to Laos. It was accepted by the Senate. The Under-Secretary of State, Elliot Richardson, promised that no ground troops would be sent to Laos without consultation with congressional leaders. The debate on the justice of American actions in Laos went on.

On February 8, 1970, the South Vietnamese Army, supported by U.S. jets, helicopter gunships, and artillery —but not ground troops—launched an invasion of Laos along Route 9 for the purpose of cutting off the flow of North Vietnamese soldiers and supplies along the Ho Chi Minh Trail into southern Laos, Cambodia, and South Vietnam. If successful, the drive would ease Communist pressure on northern parts of South Vietnam. From the American point of view, the Laotian operation would gain more time for the Saigon government to strengthen its forces and especially to permit the continued withdrawal of U.S. ground troops. The President's congressional opponents saw the operation not as a winding down of the war but as an extension.

The major supply depots and staging areas for North Vietnamese troops and Vietcong guerrillas were in eastern Cambodia, from which they slipped in and out with ease because Prince Norodom Sihanouk, the Prime Minister of the royal government of Cambodia, was favorably disposed. But when Prince Sihanouk left Cambodia on a visit to Russia, he was overthrown by a *coup d'état.*

Civil war raged on in Cambodia in 1970–1971 between the forces of the Republicans opposing Sihanouk (and their South Vietnamese allies) and the armies of Sihanouk (and his North Vietnamese allies). The latter virtually cut off the city of Phnom-Penh which was without food and fuel for a time. The Cambodian Republic's army was enlarged and trained under U.S. and South Vietnamese auspices in order to meet the expected onslaught of the enemy. When General Lon Nol appealed for aid, the United States responded by supporting his operations with air strikes while South Vietnam moved in infantry to keep open vital road links like Highway 4. The going was hard for the anti-Sihanouk forces. Communist commandoes blew up almost the whole Cambodian Air Force near Phnom-Penh.

President Nixon decided to make a military intervention in Cambodia. The two-month campaign (April 30 to June 30, 1970) was a "search-and-destroy" mission. It aimed to neutralize North Vietnamese and Vietcong sanctuaries within Cambodia which had been used for five years for attacks on South Vietnam, and so lessen the threat to Saigon and the south. Some 32,000 Americans and 48,000 South Vietnamese troops engaged the enemy in their Cambodian base areas. The President confined the operations of U.S. troops to a 21-mile limit within Cambodia. The allied forces captured thousands of weapons and ammunition, rockets, mortars, recoilless rifles, mines, explosives, vehicles, and a large supply of rice. In the process, they inflicted heavy losses on the Communist enemy. The campaign, so the President maintained, guaranteed the continuation of the troop-withdrawal program and bought time for the South Vietnamese to strengthen themselves against their Communist adversaries. He considered the operation a military success, even though North Vietnamese forces had avoided a pitched battle.

The reaction to the American venture in Cambodia was negative both at home and abroad. Protests occurred in London, Rome, West Berlin, Stockholm, Hong Kong, Manila, and Sydney, while many governments criticized the United States. At home the Cambodian invasion led to widespread anger and demonstrations, and gave new life to the antiwar movement. Students were especially militant. Protest strikes at Princeton and at other colleges virtually brought academic life to an end. Violence erupted on many campuses. The ROTC armory at the University of Maryland was ransacked. Angry confrontation occurred at Kent State University in Ohio and the National Guard was called out to quell the riots. The President reacted angrily to the student protests and he referred on May 1st to "these bums blowing up the campuses." The most tragic event was the killing of four students at Kent State on May 4th, which will be discussed in a later chapter.

For a few days it appeared that the student protest would escalate. Perhaps the turning-point against the widespread agitation came in New York City, when Mayor John V. Lindsay, in sympathy with the antiwar movement, ordered the flag atop City Hall to be flown at half-mast in memory of the four students who fell at Kent State. A member of the City Council ran up the flag however, and on May 8, 1970, during city-sponsored memorial services, a group of construction workers and others moved in against demonstrating students. A most unlikely combination of "hard hats," Wall Street brokerage house clerks and officers, and businessmen rallied in support of the flag and the President with fists and voices. The silent majority broke its silence with a vengeance. Nevertheless, the protests continued in earnest. On May 9, 1970, over 75,000 protestors, the bulk of them students, met in Washington to demand the withdrawal of all Americans from Indochina. The President paid a visit in the early morning hours to talk to some of the students at the Lincoln Memorial.

Many members of Congress voiced strong opposition to the entry of American troops into Cambodia. Both Republicans and Democrats characterized it as madness and ghastly. They were not silenced when the President promised that American forces would be withdrawn by July and that in any case they would not advance more than 21 miles into the country. On May 11, 1970, the Senate Foreign Relations Committee approved an amendment—sponsored by Senators John Sherman Cooper (Republican from Kentucky) and Frank Church (Democrat from Idaho)—to a Foreign Military Sales Bill that unless specially authorized by Congress no funds might be expended for maintaining U.S. forces in, or for air combat over, Cambodia or for assisting any country giving military help to Cambodia. In June the Foreign Military Sales Bill, now also containing a repeal of the Gulf of Tonkin resolution, passed the Senate. The House continued to debate the matter.

The protests by antiwar demonstrators and by members of Congress did not end. Hundreds of veterans, led by disabled veterans in wheelchairs, staged an impressive protest in Washington in April 1971. Some of them cast their medals and decorations onto the steps of the Capitol. Two weeks of demonstrations culminated in a march by 200,000 protestors who demanded the end of the war. Other marchers protested in Chicago and San Francisco.

The Nixon Administration took a hard line against youthful protestors. On May 2, 1971, it ordered a pre-dawn raid on an encampment by the banks of the Potomac. Mass arrests of the youths in the "May Day Tribe" followed because they had announced that their goal in Washington was to close down the government, and had erected barricades in the streets to disrupt traffic. The quick, tough measures broke up the demonstrations.

A major concern of the Congress in 1971 was an attempt to set a date for the return of all U.S. forces in Indochina. Many legislators believed that American involvement was a tragic mistake, that the United States had no vital interest in Indochina, and that in effect (as Senator Mansfield asserted) the United States had become a sort of client of South Vietnam whose government dictated in large part what Americans did. In attempting to set a time limit on the U.S. presence in Vietnam, the Congress came into constitutional conflict with the President as Commander in Chief. The struggle was between the President's powers and congressional control over appropriations. The Administration maintained that the pressure being exerted by Congress undermined its efforts to negotiate the best possible terms from the enemy and to secure the release of American prisoners, and in effect was making a just peace much more difficult to win. Late in 1970, Congress passed a military aid measure incorporating the Cooper-Church prohibition, forbidding the sending of U.S. troops or military advisers into Cambodia. But it also provided that the President could take any steps necessary to facilitate the withdrawal of U.S. forces from Vietnam or to obtain the release of prisoners of war.

In June 1971, the Senate rejected an amendment to a bill extending the draft for two years. The amendment, which had been moved by Senators George McGovern and Mark Hatfield, leading "doves," would have set December 31, 1971 as the date when all U.S. forces had to be out of Vietnam. Later that month the Senate approved the amendment of Senator Mansfield calling on the President to withdraw all troops within nine months if all American prisoners of war were returned and to negotiate with the North Vietnamese for an immediate cease-fire. After the House rejected this amendment, a conference committee of both Houses adopted a compromise that there should be a "prompt and orderly" withdrawal by "a date certain" providing U.S. prisoners were released. The President signed the bill in September 1971. A similar amendment about ending the war was incorporated in the Military Procurement Authorization Bill. Although he signed the bill, President Nixon regarded the amendment as "without binding force or effect."

The United States continued to withdraw troops even as its negotiators in Paris sought to reach an accommodation without any seeming success. It was apparent that

UPI PHOTO

A contingent of United States Marines boarding a transport ship at Da Nang, South Vietnam, April, 1971, bound for home.

the nation was desperately trying to disengage itself from a war which its people did not want and which absorbed more time and resources than the government was willing to expend.

In 1971, Australia and New Zealand withdrew many of their troops from Vietnam. By the end of the year the United States had less than 160,000 men there. Similarly the United States reduced its forces in Thailand and the Philippines, withdrew from Laos, and turned over some bases on Taiwan (Formosa) to General Chiang's government in what was obviously a policy of reducing American presence in the Pacific.

The President said in November 1971 that another 45,000 men would be withdrawn by the first of February and that U.S. forces in Vietnam were engaged only in defensive operations. For all practical purposes the ground combat role of the American army was at an end. Additional pullouts of American troops, it was announced, would depend on the intensity of enemy activity, the success of the Vietnamization program, and progress toward effecting the release of prisoners and a cease-fire. The Air Force, however, continued its bombing in support of the operations of the South Vietnamese and in interdiction of the North Vietnamese infiltration routes. Its "protective reaction raids" on missile sites and antiaircraft positions, army supplies, troop concentrations, and oil storage depots were intended to make the North Vietnamese more anxious to negotiate an end to the war. But the raids, especially the heavy raids late in December 1971, seemed to multiply the problem of retaining the support of the American people and the Congress for the war.

2.

On March 16, 1968, a platoon commanded by Lieutenant William L. Calley, Jr., of the Americal Division had swept through the hamlet of Mylai in Quang Ngai Province, South Vietnam, which allegedly was a base of operations for the Vietcong. The platoon killed men, women, and children to a number estimated at anywhere from 80 to 600. When news of the tragedy reached the American people through exposés in the press, there was shock and dismay in many quarters. The incident became the subject of investigations by the South Vietnamese, the U.S. House of Representatives and the U.S. Army.

Twenty-five officers and enlisted men were originally charged by the Army with various crimes in connection with the Mylai incident. Charges were later dropped against nineteen of these, including Major General Samuel W. Koster, commander of the Americal Division and subsequently the superintendent of the U.S. Military Academy at West Point, for allegedly concealing the incident, and Captain Ernest Medina, Calley's immediate superior.

The principal figure in the massacre was Lieutenant Calley who was charged with premeditated murder of 102 civilians and court-martialed at Fort Benning, Georgia, in November 1970. Evidence revealed that Mylai was a "free fire" zone in which any Vietnamese civilian was assumed to be hostile and, therefore, subject to being attacked. Calley admitted directing and participating in

42

the killings of the civilians, but as he explained "That was my order, sir—that was the order of the day." He asserted that he was indoctrinated to regard all Vietnamese as potential enemies, that Vietnamese children threw grenades and planted mines. Captain Medina had ordered him to destroy everything in Mylai and that anyone there should be considered as an enemy. In March 1971, Calley was convicted of premeditated murder and sentenced to life imprisonment.

There was an immediate and angry outcry against the verdict. Over 90,000 telegrams heavily in favor of clemency for Calley reached the White House. Pro-Calley rallies and petitions were common throughout the land. Many saw Calley as a scapegoat for higher-ups or as a maligned soldier who was being persecuted for doing his duty. President Nixon responded to the public clamor. He released Calley from the stockade at Fort Benning and directed that he be confined to quarters pending the appeal of the decision. A review reduced the sentence to 20 years with possible parole within seven years.

The publicity and debate surrounding the Mylai incident highlighted the erosion of morale in the armed forces. Much had happened in recent years to render the American fighting man less effective and less dedicated than he had been in the past. The bitter divisions within the nation on the merits and justice of the Indochina war had had adverse effects on the morale of American troops. The vast majority of soldiers, sailors, and airmen served loyally and obeyed orders, but a minority was a cause for anxiety. A small number of servicemen protested the war and urged the President to end the U.S.

presence in Vietnam. In October 1971, some sailors and marines of the aircraft carrier *Coral Sea* demonstrated outside the Alameda naval air base in California, protesting their impending return to the combat zone. About a fourth of the crew signed a petition to Congress opposing the war and urging Congress to stop the ship from sailing to Vietnam.

Incidents of outright mutiny in Vietnam, refusal to obey orders ranging from battlefield orders to regulations on the length of hair, addiction to heroin and other hard drugs, racial violence, the propaganda of soldier peace-activists, and a growing awareness of their rights and the determination to carry appeals to the highest officers, all indicated that the *esprit de corps* was failing.

Observers were quick to compare the condition of the U.S. Army with the French forces after their gallant but hopeless efforts to save the French empire in Indochina. The French military were convinced that their enemy was not only the elusive guerrillas but the politicians at home who played politics with their lives and with the national honor. It was too much to expect either the French or the American Army to reconcile itself to international humiliation. There was little doubt that a root cause of the Army's problem in maintaining morale and discipline lay in the American society—the changes that fragmented national purpose, the decline of patriotism in certain circles, the cult of comfort which would naturally shun the dangerous life under arms, unfulfilled expectations that led to frustration and violence, racial conflict, and civil disobedience which disposed some young people to defy authority. Another root cause was the policy of "civilianizing" the armed forces. This had turned out to mean the attraction of recruits who wanted good pay, educational benefits, opportunities to travel— in short, a rewarding job and not dedicated service to a cause. To encourage enlistments, the Army democratized itself and made lenient some of its practices, like reveille, kitchen police, and inspection. Admiral Elmo Zumwalt, Chief of Naval Operations, relaxed dress codes for enlisted men and modernized some regulations. In the process, some critics said, the forces had unwittingly undermined patriotic motives for joining up and had weakened military authority. Still another cause was a decline in the sense of dedication in the officer corps. According to this reasoning, Mylai occurred because there was a lack of military professionalism in the officers.

A number of incidents and attitudes during 1970–1971 reflected the low state of the armed forces. Unlike the servicemen who came back from Europe and Asia after World War II to a grateful nation, the veterans who returned from Vietnam were greeted with a singular lack of enthusiasm and on occasion with undisguised hostility. They felt that the nation generally did not appreciate them because the war was unpopular; that some Americans feared them on the grounds that they had behaved violently in Indochina; and that, therefore, not enough jobs or benefits awaited them.

A public outcry occurred in August 1970 when the Defense Department disposed of surplus and highly lethal nerve-gas from Army depots by loading it on a ship that would be sunk at a depth of 16,000 feet off the coast of Florida. Court challenges were unsuccessful. But the Senate passed measures tightening controls of chemical and biological-warfare agents.

Books, articles, and television programs contained harsh criticism of the military. A television documentary shown by CBS (Feb. 23 and March 23, 1971), the *Selling of the Pentagon,* detailed an expensive public relations campaign of the Department of Defense. Vice President Agnew charged that the documentary was "a clever propagandistic attempt to discredit the defense establishment." A House subcommittee voted to cite the president of CBS for refusing to provide nontelevised material pertinent to the documentary, but the House returned the recommendation to committee.

Some leaders warned that hostility toward the military would endanger national security by making Americans reluctant to pay for necessary defenses and weapons. They pointed to the Strategic Air Command's fleet of B-52 bombers, which at the end of 1971 was still an important means of delivering to enemy targets more than half of our strategical nuclear power. A great many of the B-52s, built between 1952 and 1962, were clearly deteriorating. Yet Congress was unwilling to replace the B-52s by the supersonic B-1s (each at a cost of $35 million) not only because of the expense but because it believed that missiles could replace bombers. Defense officials favored the retention of bombers as part of a three-weapons system (bombers, intercontinental ballistic missiles Polaris and Poseidon, and submarines) because they were time-tested and because they could be kept in the air for some hours and were therefore relatively free from attack.

The critical view toward war or defense-related actions that affected the public interest was seen when the Atomic Energy Commission announced that it would test, on November 6, 1971, a complex nuclear warhead for the Spartan missile in a cavern over a mile below the surface of Amchitka in the Aleutian Islands. The Spartan was part of the Safeguard missile defense system planned to intercept nuclear warheads 400 to 600 miles in space. Nationwide and even worldwide controversy and debate ensued. Environmentalists and other protestors predicted earthquakes, tidal waves, and lethal radiation from this planned underground explosion, 250 times as powerful as the bomb that leveled Hiroshima in 1945. They mounted a vigorous campaign and brought the case before the Supreme Court, which decided by 4–3 to permit the test only hours before the deadline. The test went off without incident.

FOREIGN POLICY

The basic outlines of the Nixon foreign policy emerged clearly: "winding down" the war in Southeast Asia, easing relations with Russia and especially China, and pressuring old allies to shoulder their share of the burdens of defense. This was a response to the growth in the United States of a new isolationism, to a feeling that the United States had been taken for granted too long and that the nation ought not to subordinate its interests to those of its allies in Europe and in Asia. The Nixon doctrine reflected a widespread desire to reduce American military presence where it was overextended, and to goad nations which presently depended on American troops to upgrade their own armed forces so that they could ward off subversion and guerrilla attacks.

Since the end of World War II, the United States had spent nearly $150 billion in loans and gifts to assist over one hundred other countries. Americans were now unwilling to continue such largesse. On October 29, 1971, the Senate temporarily ended the basic foreign-aid program by refusing to authorize new funds. This action was understandable in terms of the feeling that the rest of the world had taken United States aid for granted. Other reasons included the pressure on American resources, which were deemed insufficient for basic domestic needs; a general disillusionment fostered by the war in Vietnam; and resentment at what many Americans regarded as shoddy treatment of their country by foreign powers. In this connection, Americans were stunned by the expulsion from the United Nations of the Republic of China (Taiwan), an old ally, by the votes of nations which had received American aid over many years. The voting to unseat Taiwan was watched by millions of television viewers who were affronted by a victory dance led by the Tanzanian delegation in the chambers of the General Assembly to express joy at the seating of the People's Republic of China (Peking). The incident recalled the fact that little nations, like Tanzania, Bahrain, Equatorial Guinea, Fiji, and Lesotho had as much power in the General Assembly as the mightiest; and that the United States contributed nearly a third of the total United Nations outlay in 1970.

No doubt existed that Americans were more interested

in domestic affairs than in the foreign concerns which had been paramount since 1941. President Nixon, himself an opponent of the new isolationism, told a joint session of Congress in September 1971 that "the time has come to give new attention to America's own interests here at home." The mood of Americans was hostile to bearing the burdens of international pre-eminence. A turning inward, an obsession with personal concerns and with home-grown problems of youth, pollution, the "good life," and economic affairs fed the desire of many Americans to return to isolationist tendencies. Furthermore, the struggle in Indochina had produced a war-weariness that inhibited the President's response to international crises affecting U.S. interests and virtually eliminated the possibility of armed intervention, or even a heavy commitment of energies and money, to achieve a foreign goal.

In the light of this development, many European and Asian officials concluded that U.S. commitments to defend their countries against Communist aggression had become paper promises and that under the circumstances they should come to an understanding with the Soviet Union. This was one of the reasons, though by no means the only one, why the government of Willy Brandt of West Germany pursued an "Östpolitik" policy of reaching an accommodation with Moscow and its eastern European satellites. America's role in the defense of Europe, essential during the Cold War, came to a close in 1971 when a nonaggression treaty was signed between the Soviet Union and the Federal Republic of (West) Germany. The latter acknowledged Russia's control over the eastern half of Europe. In another treaty with Poland,

West Germany accepted the loss of about one-third of German lands taken by the Russians in World War II. West Germany hoped to be able to invest in the modernization of Russian technology.

The signs were many in 1970 that a shift had occurred in the balance of world power and influence. The prestige of the United States was on the wane while that of the Soviet Union was growing. The Russians had caught up with the United States in intercontinental missiles and they acted boldly in supporting Egypt against Israel. The increasing military superiority of the Russians in Europe and their growing naval presence in the Atlantic, the Mediterranean, the Middle East, and even in the Indian Ocean reflected the confidence of Moscow in dealing with the United States. The responses by Washington to certain Russian moves that years before would have called down the wrath of American diplomats were almost supine. The acquisition of bases by the Red Navy in the Indian Ocean was little noticed, while U.S. efforts to prevent a Marxist, Salvador Allende, from becoming President of Chile were spiritless and ineffective. It was clear for all to see that the hegemony of the United States was over. A Swiss official said, "For a long time the United States was the supreme ideal for all of us, but now our attitude is more realistic. The United States is neither a god nor the devil that it was. In the past, Europe expected America to do too much and the Americans were willing to do it. But now we expect less from the United States."

U.S.-European relations were especially shaken. Despite the vast number of American tourists and students in Europe, Americans seemed to be withdrawing to "fortress America." This worried Europeans, who were well aware that U.S. troops based in Europe since the end of World War II had prevented Russian domination. Many feared that the United States might apply to Europe the same idea of withdrawing troops as it had done in Southeast Asia, even though President Nixon during his European tour in October 1970 assured European leaders that he would not reduce U.S. strength below its current levels until at least 1972. That their fears were not groundless was evident from American public opinion and the views of members of Congress. Senator Mansfield, the Majority Leader, unsuccessfully proposed in the spring of 1971 to reduce the number of U.S. military personnel in Europe from 300,000 to 150,000.

President Nixon favored face-to-face diplomacy with foreign chiefs of state or government heads, at the White House, elsewhere in the United States, or abroad. In the fall of 1970 he spent nine days in brief visits to Italy (where he also visited the Pope), Yugoslavia (first American President to do so), Spain, Britain, and the Irish Republic. Along with Mrs. Nixon, Secretary of State, William Rogers and Dr. Henry Kissinger, Assistant for National Security Affairs, he was cordially received. In 1971 he met with Emperor Hirohito of Japan, Presidents Tito of Yugoslavia, Pompidou of France, and Prime Ministers McMahon of Australia, Gandhi of India, Meir of Israel, Trudeau of Canada, Heath of the United Kingdom, Sato of Japan, and Chancellor Brandt of West Germany.

In February 1970 the President submitted to Congress

a lengthy "State of the World" message entitled, *United States Foreign Policy for the 1970's—a New Strategy for Peace*. He noted that the world situation had changed drastically in recent years. Western Europe and Japan were now fully recovered from the ravages of World War II and were no longer totally dependent on American might for survival. At the same time, international Communism had lost its unity as a result of the rivalry of the Soviet Union and the People's Republic of China, who were almost coming to blows in their efforts to lead the Socialist camp and to promote their own national interests. Another recent change was the end of U.S. monopoly over nuclear weapons and the growing destructiveness of new weapons that threatened to wipe out those who employed them. As Mr. Nixon saw it, to obtain durable peace it was necessary to work in partnership with other nations, to be strong, and to be willing to negotiate differences with all nations. This did not mean that differences between the United States and the Communist world had disappeared. There were still "strong convictions and contrary philosophies, necessities of national security, and deep-seated differences of perspectives formed by geography and history."

The report acknowledged the changed position of the United States with regard to nuclear supremacy. The Nixon Administration abandoned the nuclear deterrence policy of assured destruction, which went back to the days of John Foster Dulles and Dwight Eisenhower and had been followed by the Kennedy and Johnson Administrations as well. This policy sought to prevent a missile attack on the United States by providing for a preponderant retaliatory strike that would spell suicide to the aggressor. The new American strategic goal was "sufficiency" of strategic force against possible attacks. "The balance of nuclear power has placed a premium on negotiation rather than confrontation," the President said.

The State of the World message acknowledged what many felt to be true—that U.S. forces could not be expected to put down subversion and guerrilla warfare or wars of liberation throughout the world. The way to deal with insurrections was to forestall them through economic development and social reform, and to control them by the local government that was threatened. Students of international relations and of Communism, however, doubted whether expansionist revolutionaries could be defeated without the intervention of U.S. forces.

One of the principal strains in U.S.-European relations was economic. The growing industries and trade of Europe, made more effective through the Common Market, were rivals of American business for world markets. West Germany had become an industrial giant and its currency had increased in value in relation to the dollar. Meetings between American and European officials sought to ease the economic strains. For example, President Nixon met with President Georges Pompidou of France in the Azores on December 1971 to discuss the international monetary crisis. A joint statement announced a devaluation of the dollar and the revaluation of some other currencies. The President's meeting with Prime Minister Heath of Great Britain in the same month dealt with British concern over American protectionism in trade and over the importance of keeping American troops in Europe. The President soon announced the removal of the ten percent surcharge imposed on August 15th on most imports into the United States. West German Chancellor Brandt visited Nixon at Key Biscayne, Florida, in December to discuss European and NATO problems.

American concern over the defense of Europe, though lessened, was real. In 1970, a five-year defense agreement with Spain provided for continued use by the United States of air bases at Torrejón and Saragossa and the naval base at Rota, in exchange for 120 million dollar credits to Spain for the purchase of military aircraft in the United States, 63 million dollars of appropriated funds for equipment for Spanish land forces, and finally for reciprocal defense support. In September 1970, the U.S. government announced that it would no longer withhold from Greece shipments of jet aircraft, helicopters, mortars, tanks, armored personnel carriers, and artillery. Shipments had been halted to express Washington's displeasure at the military coup in 1967 by which the "colonels" came to power in Greece.

President Nixon was anxious for an accommodation with the Soviet Union. In his State of the World message he acknowledged the "legitimate security interests" of Russia in Eastern Europe. In February 1970, an existing agreement on cultural exchanges was liberalized for two years to provide for increasing the exchange of performing-arts groups, graduate students and young instructors.

Foremost in the President's mind, insofar as Russian relations were concerned, was prevention of a clash be-

tween the world's two super powers. Discussions on safe-
guards to be observed and the curtailing of weapons pro-
ceeded slowly, but with some visible results. Late in 1969,
talks were begun about a joint draft treaty banning nuclear weapons on the sea bed. In 1970, the Treaty on the
Non-Proliferation of Nuclear Weapons, adopted by the
General Assembly of the United Nations in 1968, came
into force.

By far the most important negotiations between the
United States and the Soviet Union were the Strategic
Arms Limitations Talks (SALT) which began in Helsinki late in 1969. Their goal was mutual limitation and
eventual reduction of the strategic arensals of nuclear
weapons. The United States announced that during the
talks it would be guided by the concept of "sufficiency,"
not superiority, of the forces and weapons required to
defend itself and its allies. By the end of 1971, six
"rounds" of talks had been held at either Helsinki or
Vienna. The participants jointly announced that their
talks would concentrate on working out an agreement
for the limitation of the deployment of antiballistic missile
systems (ABMs) and on certain measures to limit offensive strategic weapons. At the fifth "round" at Helsinki,
two agreements were negotiated to reduce the risk of the
outbreak of nuclear war and to provide an improved
"hot-line" of satellite communications systems between
Washington and Moscow. The United States alleviated
the possibility of famine in the Soviet Union by selling
that nation over 250 million dollars worth of grain. This
had the effect of further driving up the price of food in
the United States.

Symbolic of the loss of prestige as well as the extremes to which the United States would go to promote Soviet friendship was the case of Simas Kudirka, a Lithuanian sailor serving on a command ship for a Soviet fishing fleet. On November 23, 1970, he leaped to freedom on to the deck of the U.S. Coast Guard cutter *Vigilant,* while both ships were moored off Martha's Vineyard, Massachusetts. Russian crewmen were permitted to drag Kudirka away, despite the fact that he sought haven in the United States. A great outcry was heard at home and abroad. President Nixon ordered "immediate remedial action to insure that there will never be a recurrence of a shocking incident of this kind."

The clashes of interest with the Soviet Union were deep and serious. Russia supported the North Vietnamese and made possible the stubborn resistance to American and South Vietnamese efforts to dislodge them in the South and return them to the North. There was rivalry in space, in the Middle East, in India and Latin America.

Russian seapower was at its zenith and becoming an offensive rather than a defensive arm of Soviet military power. As a result of the buildup that followed the Cuban missile crisis, Russian warships in the North Atlantic outnumbered those of NATO by a ratio of 6 to 1; in the Mediterranean, they exceeded the U.S. Sixth Fleet by 6 to 4. The presence of Russian warships in Egyptian and Syrian waters inhibited the Israelis; in the Persian Gulf and the Indian Ocean their presence indicated an aggressive naval strategy. The stationing of nuclear-armed Russian submarines off the east and west coasts of the United States reflected Russian confidence and poise, while the growing Russian presence in the Caribbean, supported by Cuban allies, posed a strategic threat. Russian trawlers, packed with electronic gear, plied the oceans of the world, stalked British and American vessels, observed naval maneuvers and space shots from Cape Kennedy and the recoveries in the Pacific. The Russian navy tried to offset its disadvantages: the lack of air cover at sea and the lack of better bases close to its centers of operation.

Of greater concern to the United States was the bold strategy of the Soviet Union in extending influence everywhere in the globe and especially in the Middle East. The Russians were active in the Western Hemisphere as well. They had an ally in Castro's Cuba. They signed an agreement with Chile whose Marxist president, Salvador Allende, would (they hoped) give them a base in South America. They extended a large loan to Bolivia. They even tried to develop a friendship with Canada by exploiting the political and economic differences that divided Washington and Ottawa. Canadian Prime Minister Pierre Elliott Trudeau visited Russia and P. Aleksei N. Kosygin reciprocated by coming to Canada. Possible economic cooperation was discussed.

A question, that deeply disturbed many students of Soviet affairs was whether the increase in Russian power and influence would tempt the leaders in Moscow to embark on expansionist adventures that would inevitably produce a clash with the United States. Tensions and disagreements between the two powers were many. In the fall of 1970, three U.S. and Turkish officers flew a plane by error into Soviet Armenia and were returned after a three-week detainment. Russia repeated the usual complaints about violations of Soviet airspace. Also, late in 1970, the White House announced that intelligence data indicated that Russia might be constructing a permanent submarine facility on the southern coast of Cuba, a step viewed with utmost seriousness. But Moscow retorted that no naval base would be built in Cuba. Department of Defense spokesmen later said that new evidence suggested it unlikely that a nuclear submarine base was being built in violation of the 1962 Kennedy-Khrushchev understanding that no offensive missiles be placed there.

The obstacles placed in the paths of Soviet Jews who wished to emigrate to Israel was a subject of considerable concern to their coreligionists in the United States. Demonstrations and protests were directed by American Jews against Soviet officials in New York. The Jewish Defense League (JDL), led by Rabbi Meir Kahane, and other groups kept up a steady harassment of Soviet officials in order to call attention to the plight of Russian Jews. The bombing of the New York City offices of Aeroflot, the Soviet airline and tourist agency, as well as of the Soviet cultural building in Washington, embarrassed the U.S. government. The Soviet Union reacted to JDL protests by encouraging the harassment of Americans in Moscow. JDL had also demonstrated early in 1970 against the visit to the United States by the French President, Pompidou. It asserted that the French government by selling military jets to Libya showed that it was pro-Arab and anti-Israel.

For more than a score of years the United States and Red China had been enemies. They had come to blows in Korea in 1950. The Nixon Administration now took measures to end the hostility and made overtures to the Communist masters of Peking. The basis for this change in policy might be dated in 1967, when Mr. Nixon said in an article in *Foreign Affairs* that in the long run "we simply cannot afford to leave China forever outside the family of nations, there to nurture its fantasies, cherish its hates and threaten its neighbors."

In 1969, the President had relaxed some restrictions on trade and travel to mainland China which permitted foreign subsidiaries of U.S. companies to trade with China in nonstrategic goods. In 1970, he indicated his desire to normalize relations with the Peking regime by observing that we had "historic ties of friendship with the Chinese people, and many of our basic interests are not in conflict," and that Red China should not remain isolated. In July 1970, the Chinese released the aged Bishop James Walsh, a Roman Catholic missionary who had been sentenced to prison in 1960 on trumped-up charges that he had engaged in counterrevolutionary activities. In 1971, Peking invited a U.S. table-tennis team for a visit which opened what newsmen dubbed "ping-pong diplomacy." A limited number of reporters were permitted to enter China. Meanwhile, the American public became rabidly interested in Chinese life and customs.

Although relations between Washington and Peking were steadily improving, the world was surprised to hear President Nixon's announcement that his assistant, Dr. Henry Kissinger, had secretly flown to Peking to confer with Premier Chou En-lai of the People's Republic. This took place between July 9 and 11, 1971. The Chinese extended an invitation to President Nixon to visit mainland

UPI PHOTO

Dr. Henry Kissinger, Presidential Adviser for National Security Affairs (and later Secretary of State), is greeted at the airport in Peking, People's Republic of China, during his visit there, July 9th, 1971.

China before May 1972. Although the President said that the new relationship with Peking "will not be at the expense of our old friends," the Republic of China (Taiwan), a faithful ally since World War II, objected vigorously.

A particularly thorny problem in Sino-American relations was the long effort of Communist and "neutralist" countries to seat the Chinese Communist regime in the United Nations and to expel the Republic of China, headed by Generalissimo Chiang Kai-shek. American diplomats were in the awkward position of trying to keep the Taiwan government in the United Nations while wooing the People's Republic, which proclaimed that it would not take a seat in the United Nations as long as its archenemy, Taiwan, was a member. In the fall of 1971, Washington supported a plan for dual representation for Taiwan and Peking. One of the five permanent seats in the Security Council would go to the People's Republic, while a seat in the General Assembly would be retained by the Republic of China. In a debate that was very disturbing to Americans, the Assembly disregarded the American plea by expelling Taiwan. Many old allies deserted the United States. Japan was among the handful supporting Washington.

The thaw in the Cold War between Washington and Peking presaged a sweeping realignment of power in Asia and the world and helped to shatter the international structures following World War II. The Soviet Union, suspicious of Peking, feared a close Chinese-American understanding. Japan and other free nations of the East realized that the Sino-American accommodation and the Nixon doctrine would force them to take more active roles in their own security and that of their neighbors, that they could not automatically count on Washington as a world policeman. It was even possible that Japan would now forsake her old alliance with the United States and ally herself with Russia or China. The ending of China's self-imposed isolation was likely to have even greater consequences in the years to come.

In 1970 the U.S.-Japanese Security Treaty was extended. Its provisions pledged the United States to defend Japan against aggressors and the Japanese government to provide the necessary bases for American forces stationed in the Japanese islands. In June 1971, the United States and Japan signed an agreement for the return to Japan in the following year of Okinawa and the other Ryukyu Islands which American troops had occupied since World War II. Japan granted the United States the use of some bases in the Ryukyus in accordance with the Treaty of Mutual Cooperation and Security of 1960. Whatever good will might have accompanied the return of the islands was lost when President Nixon failed to consult Tokyo prior to reaching his decision to visit Peking, and when he levied a ten percent surcharge on American imports which struck hard at Japanese products.

Economic and financial differences drove a wedge between the two nations. Japan had become in the post-World War II period the third greatest industrial state. Unlike the United States which had to shoulder heavy defense burdens for itself and for many countries, Japan was able to direct all its energies to production and world trade. Success greeted Japanese efforts to sell automobiles, electronic equipment, appliances, cameras, and textiles. Parallel efforts of American businessmen to tap Japanese markets met various trade and investment barriers. The result was that Americans bought far more from Japan than they were able to sell in Japan. An annual one-billion dollar deficit had built up over the last five years. American dollars flowed into Japan. The task of reversing an unfavorable balance of trade was hard. Requests made by Washington to remove trade barriers, to revaluate the Japanese currency, to build up defense forces in order to remove part of the burden from the backs of American taxpayers all strained friendship.

When India and Pakistan were formed in 1947, the latter was a two-part country—East Pakistan and West Pakistan—separated by 1000 miles of Indian territory. The two new nations were at sword's point from the beginning. Disputes going back centuries, over religion, territories, customs and race, divided India and Pakistan and also East and West Pakistan. The divisions within Pakistan gave India the opportunity to exploit the weaknesses of her rival. The Bengalis of East Pakistan were alienated and felt neglected by the West Pakistan government.

The immediate origins of the conflict between the two parts of Pakistan went back to elections in December 1970 when a majority of seats in the National Assembly went to the Awami League, primarily representing East Pakistan, and hostile to the military regime of General Mohammed Yahya Khan. When he delayed the convening of the Assembly, East Pakistan erupted in revolt and declared its independence as Bangla Desh, with its capital at Dacca. India actively supported the rebels. The Pakistani army, composed largely of West Pakistani soldiers, invaded the East. A savage guerrilla war followed, with extensive civilian casualties. East Pakistan was a scene of desolation. The war added to the disasters of a cyclone in November 1970 that resulted in floods and famine. Refugees, perhaps over nine million, fled the famine and the fighting and crossed over into India.

The stage was set for another war between India and Pakistan (they had fought in 1965 over Kashmir). Indian troops moved toward East Pakistan's frontier. Clashes began in November and soon there was full-scale war. India won a quick and smashing victory and Bangla Desh made good its claim to independence.

Events on the Indian subcontinent became matters of national dispute in the United States. Senator Edward Kennedy (Democrat from Massachusetts) accused the Pakistani army of genocide against the people of East Pakistan—a point disputed by others. Greater concern was expressed for the victims of war and famine. Americans, either personally or through organizations, joined with others throughout the world in sending food and supplies to East Pakistan.

The tensions leading to conflict and the war itself involved the United States. The White House unsuccessfully tried to head off the conflict. India did not look to Washington for support; she had the attention of Moscow which had been wooing her for years. India and Russia signed a twenty-year friendship pact in August 1971. The Soviet Union came to the aid of her friend not only by pouring in military aid but by strong support in the United Nations. The UN was hopelessly inadequate to effect a cease-fire. The efforts of the Security Council to order India and Pakistan to lay down their arms were frustrated by Russian vetoes, which were intended to secure enough time for India to achieve a crushing military victory.

The United States suspended military aid to India on December 1, 1971, having already done so for Pakistan. An American official said at the outbreak of the war that the major responsibility rested with India because she chose a military solution to the political problem in East Pakistan. On December 15, Mrs. Indira Gandhi, the Indian Prime Minister, told Mr. Nixon that, "We are deeply hurt by innuendoes and insinuations that it was we who have precipitated the crisis, or in any way thwarted or hindered a solution." The U.S. Seventh Fleet left the Gulf of Tonkin off Vietnam and steered for the Bay of Bengal. Soviet ships also sailed to Indian waters.

The Indian-Pakistani struggle altered the international balance. Soviet influence grew while American prestige dipped. The reasons for the support of Pakistan by Washington were clear. As American efforts to woo India failed and Soviet influence grew at New Delhi, the Nixon Administration had to back Pakistan. To have supported India would still have left the United States subordinate to the Soviet Union which was prepared to go all out for her new ally. Besides, to have backed India would have meant the end of the military agreements already in force with Pakistan. An additional powerful motive was that Pakistan had fallen within the sphere of influence of Red China, with whom the United States wished to come to terms. It seemed that Washington would have to suffer a diplomatic defeat in India to achieve its long-range purposes.

The Middle East was a source of sharp rivalry and some cooperation between the United States and the Soviet Union. The growing presence of Russian naval and military forces was a threat to the United States and her ally Israel. Bilateral U.S.-Soviet talks on maintaining peace between Israel and her Arab neighbors continued late in 1969. The American formula was simply the withdrawal of Israeli forces from Arab territories taken in the 1967 war, with an Arab assurance of a binding peace commitment. Neither the Soviet Union and its Egyptian ally nor Israel accepted the proposals.

It appeared that war might erupt at any moment along Israel's borders. Arab commandoes raided Israeli villages and installations from bases inside Jordan and Lebanon, whose governments had little control over these guerrillas. This led to Israeli retaliatory raids against the terrorists and against Jordan and Lebanon. The hundreds of thousands of Palestinian refugees, displaced by the Israelis in establishing their state, longed to return to their homes. They brooded in primitive camps that lacked the least comforts. It was easy to recruit guerrillas from these angry people who would not reconcile themselves to the existence of Israel. The threat to peace came not only from the guerrilla raids and Israeli retaliation, but also from Israeli raids over the Suez Canal. Public opinion in many lands became alienated to Israel.

Israelis charged that their supremacy over the skies of the Middle East was threatened by the Russian decision to equip Egypt with SAM-3 missiles and their general security by the powerful military and naval forces stationed in Egypt (the United Arab Republic). Thousands of Russian technicians and advisers were helping Egyptians to operate sophisticated equipment and weapons, while Russian pilots flew operational missions in the area.

In March 1970, Secretary of State William Rogers announced a delay in the sale of *Phantom* and *Skyhawk* military planes to Israel unless the balance of power changed to Israel's disadvantage. He regarded the strengthening of Egyptian defenses with the SAM-3 missiles as being defensive. Americans continued to press for negotiations. On August 7, 1970, Egypt, Jordan, and Israel accepted Rogers' proposal to observe a 90-day cease-fire. During this period Rogers believed that the three warring powers would settle their differences through the good offices of Dr. Gunnar Jarring, the UN mediator. The United States hoped that Israel would withdraw from the Arab lands occupied in 1967, and that in return the Arab States would recognize Israeli independence and security. Four permanent members of the Security Council (United States, Soviet Union, United Kingdom, and France) formally approved the American peace initiative.

Peace talks took place at UN headquarters in New York. The Arab world was not united on the decision of Egypt and Jordan to negotiate with Israel. Syria, Iraq, and the Palestinian guerrilla groups like *Al Fatah* rejected the U.S. proposals. A month after the cease-fire, Israel broke off the talks because Egyptians were moving their Russian-built missiles closer to the Suez Canal and

thereby threatening Israeli air superiority there. Reluct-
antly, Washington supported Israel. Talks with Jarring
resumed in January 1971 but were inconclusive because
Israel would not promise to withdraw from occupied
Arab lands before negotiations resumed. Meanwhile, in
September 1970, American, Swiss, and British airliners
were hijacked by Arab commandoes of the Popular Front
for the Liberation of Palestine, flown to a guerrilla-con-
trolled airstrip in Jordan, and destroyed—an incident discussed in a later chapter.

The guerrillas were a state within a state. When King
Hussein ordered the Jordanian Army to crack down on
the Palestinian commandoes, a bloody fight followed.
The United States was ready to move in some forces to
protect American citizens and to warn Russia, but this
measure was not necessary. Peacemaking between Hussein and the guerrillas fell to the Egyptian President,
Gamal Abdel Nasser, who used his considerable prestige
to bring about an accommodation. The Jordanian crisis
convinced Washington to send additional jets to Israel
and to Jordan.

Washington doubled its efforts to secure peace in the
Middle East in 1971. Secretary of State Rogers implored
Israel to withdraw to her pre-1967 boundaries in exchange for "adequate, satisfactory" arrangements in Sinai
and at Sharm-el-Sheikh guaranteed by an international
peace force of a continuing nature. And he pledged that
the United States would play a leading role in guarantee-
ing Israel's security. The Israelis, however, would not
pull back their forces from the east bank of the Suez
Canal, still closed to shipping. They maintained that be-

fore they would return lands seized in 1967 they wanted first a peace treaty incorporating defensible frontiers and the recognition of Jerusalem as their capital. The UN called on Israel to rescind the changes it had already made in the status of Jerusalem. Rogers visited five Middle East countries for discussions with Arab and Israeli leaders in May 1971. There followed visits by senior American diplomats to Cairo for talks with Egyptian leaders on the best way of opening the Canal.

Israel emphasized to the American government and to the news media the dangers to her and the United States of increased Russian participation in Egyptian affairs. Following the visit of President Sadat (who succeeded Nasser) to Moscow, a Soviet-Egyptian communiqué (October 1971) noted Russia's intention of taking measures aimed at further increasing Egypt's military strength. U.S. Senators, at once, overwhelmingly urged President Nixon immediately to resume sending F-4 *Phantom* fighter-bombers to Israel.

THE NATIONAL ECONOMY

I.

The 1970 Census revealed that the total population of the United States on April 1st was 204,765,770, which was an increase of over 23,800,000 since 1960. The growth rate of 13.4 percent was next to the lowest in American history—yet a number of population experts still advocated "population growth zero," that is no increase or even a decline in the population in order to conserve what some deemed to be dwindling world natural resources. California grew by some 27 percent in the 1960's and surpassed New York as the most populous state, thereby gaining five additional seats in the House of Representatives. Pennsylvania, Texas (which moved up from sixth place to fourth), and Illinois followed. Almost one-sixth of the population live in a narrow belt of land from Washington to Boston, the so-called Northeast Corridor. The Census also revealed that of the twenty-five largest cities, thirteen had lost population to the suburbs. However, twenty-four of the twenty-five largest metropolitan areas, that include the city proper and the surrounding urban and suburban districts, gained in population. The New York metropolitan area numbered 11,410,000. Los Angeles-Long Beach, California (greater than Chicago) was 6,962,000. For the first time in national history, more Americans lived in the suburbs than in the cities. Contrary to opinion, suburban areas came close to or even surpassed cities in the number of jobs they provided. In the largest metropolitan areas, jobs shifted to the suburbs. Only one out of four workers in the suburbs commuted to a city job. For the first time since Reconstruction, the South gained more people through migration than it lost to the Northeast, Midwest, and West. The West grew rapidly. Nevada, for example, gained over 70 percent; Arizona, more than 36 percent.

In the midst of great affluence, however, there were pockets of poverty. In 1971, the Bureau of the Census reported that 25.5 million Americans lived "below the poverty line." This poverty line was defined for a nonfarm family of four in 1970 as an annual income of $3,968 or less (excluding income from sale of property, borrowed funds, gifts, lump-sum inheritances and lump-sum insurance payments). The poverty line admittedly was set higher here than in many parts of the world.

A third of all blacks lived below the official poverty-income level, as compared to a tenth of whites. But in total numbers, whites constituted 70 percent of the poverty population.

The concern of Americans over economic crises diverted their attention from their amazing material prosperity since World War II. The standard of living that they deemed adequate in 1970 would have been seen as a dream in 1945. In contrast to most of the people of the world, Americans enjoyed advantages that could only make others envious.

The total output of goods and services (GNP) in 1971 dollars was $1,059 billion, up 138 percent since 1946. The average annual family income before taxes was $10,300, up 77 percent since 1946. The number of households owning homes almost doubled in that period. Americans owned about 90 million television sets and about 64 million refrigerators (almost a 200 percent increase since 1946). Whereas only about half of the American families owned an automobile after World War II, in 1971 some 80 percent did. The total value of savings accounts in financial institutions increased sevenfold to over 448 billion. Over 80 percent of American families have at least one member covered by life insurance. About 183 million people are protected in some fashion by hospitalization insurance.

Despite the fact that wide disparities in the distribution of income persisted, some 12 million households reported an income of $15,000 or more, as compared to only 1.5 million households in 1950 (but this figure should be qualified by noting that three-fourths of all households had more than one paycheck).

Part of the gain in the GNP resulted from inflation. Nevertheless, in 1971 the United States produced as much goods and services as it had from 1789 to the mid-1870's. In 1970, it produced more than twice as much as West Germany, France, Italy, Belgium, Netherlands, and Luxembourg combined. Although it occupies only seven percent of the world's land area and has about six percent of the world population, the United States possesses about half the productive power of the rest of the world combined. The physical plant of the U.S. economy is valued at more than $2,500,000,000,000 five times what it was in 1900.

2.

Part of the increase in the annual output of the nation's goods and services (GNP) was due to rampant inflation which in turn was an effect of heavy expenditures for the war in Southeast Asia and for the "Great Society" programs of former President Lyndon Johnson who had been of the opinion that the economy could support both a major war and social benefits to millions of Americans; in short, that the United States could have both guns and butter.

Specific details are indicative of the behavior of the economy during 1970 and 1971. Prices fell sharply on

Wall Street in May 1970 and underwent additional severe fluctuation during the summer. Industry trimmed or shelved its expansion plans; sales fell off; consumers deferred spending; the higher costs of borrowing money squeezed many businesses and local governments; and business failures mounted. The most spectacular was the bankruptcy of the Penn Central Railroad in June 1970.

The economy was also weakened by the 67-day General Motors strike in the fall of 1970, which directly affected 340,000 workers and also the glass, steel, and automobile-parts industries. All told, the loss to the GNP was about $8 billion.

Inflation disrupted the economy, contributing largely to labor unrest, frequent strikes, growing unemployment, shrinking corporate profits, and increasing bankruptcies. The typical American saw its main effect in the high cost of living. Food prices soared and the cost of eating-out resulted in his shunning the more expensive restaurants, dining at home, and patronizing the "fast food" establishments that dotted the principal highways and shopping centers.

Yet for the period 1961–1971, while food prices rose 29 percent, clothing 33 percent, physicians fees 64 percent, and daily room-rates in hospitals 165 percent, salaries and wages rose by 100 percent. The prime cause of the price increases was the amount of money that Americans could spend on food, other necessities, and on luxuries. The increases in food prices were also due to the increased demand in Europe and in Japan for American grain (used to feed animals). The huge foreign and domestic demand for feed grains—called "meat-by-the-bushel"—led to soaring prices. Still, while food took 16 percent of income after taxes in 1961, it took 12.7 percent in 1971.

As compared to a score of years before, the dollar of 1971 was only worth 65 cents. According to one estimate, the consumer had to earn at least one-fourth more than he did five years before to make up for the increased cost of living and for taxes. Workers discovered that their raises were wiped out by inflation. Retired people realized that their fixed incomes were insufficient for adequate housing, food and medical care. Businessmen saw their profit margins shrink or disappear; and farmers knew that their larger gross incomes were depleted by spiraling costs for machinery, cattle feed, insecticides, and taxes. The small farmer's special complaint was that the government and the country as a whole ignored his problems. In fact, most Americans suffered. As one study found, inflation "takes something from everyone's real income" but "the poorest and the richest lose the most to inflation."

Unemployment became a bane of the Nixon Administration by passing the four percent figure that experts considered normal for "full employment." At one point it surpassed six percent. In 1971, while the rate for adult men was 4.4 percent, it was higher for black workers and also, for teenagers and married women. It was very high for unskilled workers or for those whose skills were no longer needed because of technological or economic changes. Certain pockets of high unemployment like Seattle, Washington, which reflected the losses of the Boeing Aircraft Company, were vexing for government and union officials.

Joblessness not only affected the unskilled and the blue-collar workers but also white-collar workers, managers and executives. To their surprise and shock, scientists and engineers lost their positions because of the cutbacks in the aerospace and defense programs. Some spoke of the "science depression." Many recent college graduates were unable to find suitable positions in their fields, and a number of professions like college teaching were overstaffed.

Government assistance was increased. In 1971, the rules of the Federal food stamp program permitted the addition of another 1.75 million persons and the availability of free stamps to any family of four whose monthly income is clearly minimal. It is estimated that in 1971 almost seven percent of the population participated in all the food programs. Also, in July 1971 the Emergency Employment Act provided $2.2 billion for 150,000 jobs—the first public employment legislation since the WPA during the depression of the 1930's.

The Nixon Administration had decided in 1969 to "cool down" the economy. The Federal Reserve Board imposed monetary and fiscal restraints, and when the business decline became steeper, it eased credit restrictions in 1970. In mid-November the Board lowered the discount rate and thus made money more available so that corporations could borrow money at lower interest rates and thereby expand business activity and jobs.

The President did not regard himself responsible for having caused the recession; rather, he considered it as an evil inherited from the Johnson Administration. He saw the prosperous economy of the 1960's as a synthetic prosperity dependent on Vietnam, and as a period of catapulting wholesale prices. At the end of 1970, Mr. Nixon maintained that in the first two years of his Administration he had tried to fight inflation by holding down Federal spending and balancing the budget; the inflationary psychology, however, fed on itself and in the process had endangered the position of the dollar in the world money market. The reduction in the size of the armed forces in Vietnam and of defense production eased the inflationary pressure, which was more powerful than anyone knew. He maintained that he had slowed down a runaway inflation without bringing about recession or impeding the potential for growth in the economy. The "dangerously rising momentum of inflation was arrested by late 1969, and the rate of inflation has been moving gradually downward in 1970." The worst was over, he believed.

The Administration wanted to cut down government spending, despite heavy pressure for increasing expenditures for social programs. Although the Federal budget was in balance until mid-1970, it did not reflect the heavy borrowing of billions of dollars by Federal agencies not included in the budget. This led to further inflation. Balancing of the budget was dropped; in November 1970, in order to stimulate the economy to resume its growth, Mr. Nixon approved a budget deficit. This was the Government's "way of picking up the check for a slowdown of inflation." The Federal Reserve Board enlarged the supply of money by reducing the discount rate.

For a while the Government sought to lower wage and price levels through persuasion, "jawboning," as President Johnson had called the use of powerful suasion by government. The Council of Economic Advisers published two inflation alerts on August 8 and December 1, 1970, and pointed to certain industries as leading in the wage-and-price increase spiral.

Dissatisfied with economic progress and the rate of recovery from what he did not wish to call a recession, the President took more energetic measures. After consulting advisers like John Connally (Secretary of the Treasury), Dr. Arthur Burns (Chairman of the Federal Reserve Board), Dr. Paul McCracken (Chairman of the President's Council of Economic Advisers), and Dr. George Schultz (Director of the Office of Management and Budget), the President announced corrective measures which were based on the authority Congress had given him in May 1971 to establish wage-and-price controls. The outlines of the New Economic Program were sketched in his televised message of August 15th. He temporarily lifted the free convertibility of the dollar into gold; imposed a ten percent surcharge on about half of American imports; froze wages, rents, and prices for ninety days; announced a tax credit for investment in new equipment; requested the repeal of the excise tax on new domestic automobiles and the advance by one year of the income tax reduction scheduled to go into effect on January 1, 1973; postponed revenue-sharing with the States and welfare changes; made some Federal expenditure cuts; and created a Cost of Living Council with the responsibility of administering the "freeze" and recommending other measures. He hoped that these measures would make American goods more competitive in the world market. Concluding that the dollar was so greatly overvalued that it hurt the country's balance of trade, the President temporarily abandoned fixed parities and permitted the dollar to "float," that is, to find its true value regardless of fixed parities.

Confidence in the dollar eroded abroad. Many foreign holders of dollars exchanged them for stronger currencies like the West German mark, which had the effect of further depressing the value of the dollar in relation to the currencies of other countries. A monetary crisis was full grown by May 1971. Large U.S. imports, heavy expenditures abroad, and large investments throughout the world meant that dollars flowed out of the United States and American gold reserves dwindled. Many individuals and firms overseas had claims on U.S. gold, and Euro-dollars. Concluding that the dollar was overvalued in relation to the main trading currencies, they exchanged their Euro-dollars for the West German mark and other strong currencies.

The weakening of the dollar and the ten percent surcharge on imports into the United States were matters of grave concern for other nations, who urged that the dollar be devalued so that they need not support it. And they resented the surcharge because it made their goods more expensive in American markets. Strains increased between the United States and old allies. The Canadians, for example, enjoyed a favorable trade position with their southern neighbor and were determined to keep it.

Financial and trade talks led to a partial settlement of

the economic disputes. In his meeting with President Pompidou of France in mid-December 1971, Mr. Nixon agreed to work toward "a prompt realignment of the exchange rates through a devaluation of the dollar and revaluation of some other currencies," and announced that the seven percent investment credit was no longer restricted to U.S.-purchased equipment and machinery. Later, at a meeting with British Prime Minister Heath at Bermuda, the President agreed to the immediate lifting of the import surcharge.

The Group of Ten countries (Belgium, Canada, France, West Germany, Italy, Japan, the Netherlands, Sweden, United Kingdom, and the United States) met in Washington in the middle of December 1971 to realign the exchange rates of their currencies. They agreed to raise the dollar price of gold by about 8.5 percent from $35 to $38 per ounce, to lift the ten percent surcharge announced by Mr. Nixon in August, to realign the currency exchange rates, and to reduce restrictions on trade. By this "Smithsonian Agreement," the Americans agreed to propose to Congress the devaluation of the dollar—the first devaluation since 1934—and to reestablish fixed parities between the dollar and other currencies.

The devaluation was accomplished by an increase in the price of gold from $35 to $38 and through the restatement of the value of other currencies like the German mark and the Japanese yen in relation to the dollar. The devaluation had the effect of making American goods more competitive in price with those of other countries. It also meant that Americans would pay more for imported goods and for foreign travel.

79

Although no immediate threat existed to the dominant economic position of the United States, there were indications of a decline in America's relative place in the world's markets. The American share of exports had dropped during the last decade, while that of the European Common Market (which Britain joined) and of Japan rose sharply. What led to the decline was the remarkable recovery of former enemy nations—Japan, Germany, and Italy; the success of many countries, including the emerging nations, in growing their own food; the trade barriers to American farm products; inflation which priced U.S. goods out of the world market; and the flood of foreign products, like shoes, textiles, business machines, and automobiles, on the American domestic market. In 1969, the United States had enjoyed a trade surplus of three billions, but two years later it had the first crude trade deficit since 1888, one which depleted the gold stock and reserves. Strong sentiment was accordingly expressed by some legislators for the adoption of a more protectionist trade policy. In the 91st Congress, the House passed a bill with protectionist provisions, but the Senate did not agree.

The Nixon Administration's economic remedies had not produced the desired results. In the face of the persistent recession, the President announced additional measures to combat inflation through the "Phase Two" program announced on October 7, 1971. He appointed a Price Commission to hold down prices and rent increases and to slow down inflation, and a Pay Board to monitor wage and salary increases. Both groups were backed by the sanctions of the Cost of Living Council, though the

President said he would rely primarily on good faith and cooperation. Congress extended the President's power to regulate dividends, prices, and wages until April 30, 1973.

To stimulate the economy and win popular support, the Administration increased government spending. About $1 billion more a month would be poured into spending programs in the form of increased crop subsidies, and maximum pay raises for Federal workers within the Phase Two guidelines. Congressional opponents and State and local leaders urged the President to end his "freezing" of nearly $13 billion appropriated by Congress for highway construction, public housing, model cities, and other programs, and challenged his authority to do so.

Another measure was the lowering of interest rates by the Federal Reserve System, which had the result of pouring money into the banking system that could be used for business expansion. The Administration's new measures meant larger Federal deficits. Conservative supporters of the President were appalled at the largest budget deficits since World War II and at his abandonment of the principles of the free market. His "pump priming" measures indicated that he was following the monetary ideas of John Maynard Keynes, who had maintained that large government expenditures could stimulate the economy—ideas which conservatives in the Democratic and Republican parties had roundly denounced since New Deal days.

The recession brought in its wake demands for greater controls over industry, such as limits on prices and

UPI PHOTO

Ralph Nader, consumer advocate, speaks to the American Association for Comprehensive Health Planning at a meeting in New Orleans, December, 1971. Senator Russell B. Long, of Louisiana, first on left, is an interested listener.

profits. There was also a more generalized distrust of American business, private enterprise and property, the profit motive, and other institutions that had forged U.S. economic might. This distrust was encouraged on campuses and in the pulpits. James M. Roche of General Motors charged that some young Americans were overly critical of economic institutions and were making "an assault on the reputation of America." Attacks were leveled at the quality of consumer products, on "truth in advertising," on industrial pollution, and on corporations for not taking the lead in social reform. A term frequently heard, that covered many complaints, was that business brought down the "quality of life." In rebuttal, business leaders asserted that much of industrial pollution, automobile congestion, and accidents were themselves products of industrialization and of the extension of creature-comforts demanded by the people for the "good life"; and that they were the by-products of an economy that produced goods and services for mass markets and not for the well born and the powerful alone.

There was little doubt that business was suspect. The several layers of government increasingly immersed themselves in consumer affairs, while some individuals —notably Ralph Nader, regarded by friends as the consumer's advocate but by others as a meddler—investigated business and lobbied for regulative legislation at every level.

THE JUDICIARY

Distrust and resentment of the judiciary was expressed by many who lamented what local, State, and Federal courts had done in the field of criminal justice. Esteem for the courts, especially the U.S. Supreme Court, was eroded by claims that the courts "coddled" wrongdoers, "handcuffed" the police, granted undue delays and appeals to the accused, and imposed light sentences which were out of proportion to the gravity of the crimes. In general, the charge was that the courts tilted the balance in favor of the criminal and against society. Courtroom delays and cumbersome legal machinery did in fact hamper law enforcement. Chief Justice Burger admitted the need for court reform, that is, the introduction of more modern methods, the reexamination of prisons with a view to improving the education and rehabilitation of prisoners, the speeding up of justice, and a search for a just way of limiting the right of appeal. He outlined his concern and some of his ideas in the first "state of the judiciary" address to the annual meeting of the American Bar Association in August 1971.

The judiciary was viewed by many as responsible for busing of school children outside their neighborhoods for the purpose of achieving racial balance. An oft-repeated criticism was that the high court was too "activist" and that the Warren Court had forgotten what Justice Brandeis had warned against: that justices should not advance their own economic or social views and must not forget that the making of law belongs to the several legislatures. The Burger Court had moved away somewhat from the judicial activism of the Warren Court. Chief Justice Burger renounced the "intriguing idea" and "alluring prospect" that "our world can be changed in the courts." He went on, "those who would look to judges, and especially tenured Federal judges, to innovate and reshape our society will do well to ponder what remedy is available if the world shaped by judicial process is not to their liking." Some evidence that the Court was moving in the direction of setting limits on the rights of suspects came in *Harris v. New York* (1971), where by a 5-4 margin the Court held that statements made by a suspect could be introduced to impeach his testimony at trial, though he had not been warned of his right to remain silent and his right to counsel.

After the Senate rejected his nomination of Clement F. Haynsworth, Jr., to fill the vacancy created by the resignation of Justice Fortas, the President named George H. Carswell of Florida, a Circuit Court of Appeals judge. Strong opposition to Carswell sprang up on the grounds that he was "racist" and that he lacked the necessary qualifications. The Senate rejected him in April 1970 by a 51-45 vote. This meant that for part of the 1970 term the Court had only eight justices. The President's third choice for the Fortas vacancy, Harry A. Blackmun of Minnesota, was approved by the Senate in May 1970 with no negative votes.

Several days after the rejection of Carswell, the House Minority Leader, Gerald R. Ford, said that a bipartisan group would seek an investigation of the fitness of Justice William O. Douglas, who had been one of the Court's most controversial figures since his appointment in 1939 by Franklin D. Roosevelt. Douglas' opponents asserted that his links or sympathies with gamblers, pornographers, and radicals (in 1970 he published *Points of Rebellion* which gave every appearance of justifying revolutionary action) rendered him unfit for the Court and therefore subject to impeachment. But his friends and admirers prevailed. The chairman of the House Judiciary Committee, Emmanuel Celler, blocked the creation of the special group demanded by Ford and instead assigned the task to a subcommittee which he chaired and which predictably voted against impeachment.

In nominating Lewis F. Powell, Jr., of Virginia and William H. Rehnquist of Arizona to fill the vacancies created by the retirements of John M. Harlan and Hugo Black in September 1971, Mr. Nixon explained the basis of his selections. His nominations would go to persons who were among the very best lawyers in the nation and were judicial conservatives (those who saw the duty of the judge as the interpretation of the Constitution and were not inclined to place themselves above or outside it). "He [the nominee] should not twist or bend the Constitution in order to perpetuate his personal political and social views," the President said. He recalled his campaign pledge to nominate to the high bench those who shared his conservative judicial philosophy. Some decisions had gone too far, he continued, in weakening the peace forces coping with criminal elements. Powell, the former head of the American Bar Association, and Rehnquist, the Assistant Attorney General, met his requirements.

The battle for approval of the nominations, though

not as severe as the struggles to confirm Haynsworth and Carswell, was nevertheless spirited, especially in the case of Rehnquist. Some liberals condemned him for not revering or understanding the Bill of Rights as they interpreted it. They were upset over the President's consistent selection of conservatives and his apparent success in changing the direction of the Court. The Senate, however, approved both nominations in December 1971.

In 1970–1971, the Supreme Court dealt with many important cases and issues. The tactics of disruption in the courtroom which were being utilized by political radicals (notably in the trial of the "Chicago Seven" before Judge Julius J. Hoffman) were widely reprobated. The Supreme Court dealt with the issue of courtroom behavior in reversing a U.S. Court of Appeals decision that if a defendant was barred from the courtroom because of his disruptive behavior, he was being deprived of his right to be present. In *Illinois v. Allen* (1970), the High Court set down three possible ways to deal with an obstreperous defendant: binding and gagging him in the courtroom; citing him for contempt; or removing him and conducting the trial *in absentia* until his conduct improved.

In the case of *In re Winship* (1970), dealing with the practice of New York courts of deciding the guilt of a minor on the preponderance of evidence, the court held that a juvenile cannot be adjudged a delinquent unless the alleged crimes are proved beyond a reasonable doubt. Although Chief Justice Burger in his dissent said that the majority's decision blurred the differences between juvenile and traditional criminal courts, Justice Brennan for the majority asserted that the decision need not impair the individualized treatment accorded to young offenders.

In February 1970, the court extended its rule of "one-man-one-vote." In *Hadley v. the Junior College District of Metropolitan Kansas City* it said, "when members of an elected board are chosen from elected districts each district must be established on the basis which will insure as far as is practicable, that equal numbers of voters can vote for proportionally equal numbers of officials." But it softened its position somewhat by June 1971 in *Abate v. Mundt,* in which it upheld the apportionment of the Rockland County (New York) Board of Supervisors, though there was a population disparity of 11.9 percent between the largest and the smallest districts. Justice Marshall wrote that the deviation did not violate the equal protection clause because of the "long history, and a perceived need for, close cooperation between the county and its constituent towns," and that the practices contained no built-in bias designed to favor particular interests or geographic areas.

A very important case concerned the lowering of the voting age to eighteen. When he signed the Voting Rights Bill in June 1970, which made persons eighteen years old eligible in all elections, President Nixon alluded to some doubts about its constitutionality and to the fact that he had ordered the Justice Department to seek a court test. Four States challenged its constitutionality before the High Court, which held by a 5–4 vote that Congress was within its powers to lower the voting age in Federal elections but not in State and local elections. The

Court, however, by unanimous vote upheld the requirements abolishing literacy tests and (with only one dissent) residence requirements of more than thirty days.
(In some States, voters rejected proposals for permitting
eighteen-year-olds to vote in State and local elections.)
In order to remove all constitutional doubts, Congress
passed a constitutional amendment lowering the voting
age in March 1971, which was quickly ratified by the
States and became the 26th Amendment.

The war in Southeast Asia was the subject of many
cases in one form or the other. In January 1970, the
Court deprived the more than 4000 draft boards of the
power to accelerate induction as a disciplinary or vindic-
tive measure against men who turned in their draft cards
in protest against the war, or to deprive students of their
deferments as punishment for antiwar acts without first
giving them an opportunity to challenge the action in
court. In the Welsh case, decided in June 1970, the Court
held by 5–3 that the exemption from military service,
given in the Military Selective Service Act of 1967 to
men who are opposed to war by reason of religious training and belief, also applied to a conscientious objector
who had deeply held moral or ethical beliefs about wars
which were not necessarily of a religious nature. The new
director of Selective Service, Curtis William Tarr, set
guidelines for draft boards dealing with conscientious objection, including provisions that young men applying for
that status should be opposed to all wars, not only the war
in Vietnam, and that their views must be the result of
some kind of rigorous training and not merely a personal
moral code. In March 1970, the Court held by 8–1 that

the freedom of religion clause in the First Amendment did not confer conscientious objector status on a draftee who opposes only a particular war.

The attack on the war increasingly took the form of challenging its constitutionality (i.e., that Congress had not declared war and therefore the American involvement in Indochina was "illegal") and of disclosing to the press by means of Congressional hearings or "leaks" the nature and extent of the U.S. role since the early 1960's. Antiwar protestors hoped that the Supreme Court would hold the war to be unconstitutional.

The Massachusetts Legislature, responding to the deep antiwar sentiment of the academic communities in New England, passed a bill (April 1970) which provided that unless Congress declared war, servicemen from that State might refuse to take part in armed hostilities which were not an emergency and "not otherwise authorized in the powers granted to the President as Commander-in-Chief." The Attorney-General of Massachusetts was required to defend and protect the legal rights of such servicemen before the courts. In *Massachusetts v. Laird,* the Court dismissed the suit which dealt with the issue of the constitutionality of the war.

One of the most important cases in modern times related to the so-called "Pentagon Papers." World attention was focused on a publication in June and July 1971 by the *New York Times,* the *Washington Post,* and other newspapers of summaries and extracts from a "top-secret-sensitive," 47 volume study of American participation in Vietnam from 1945 to 1968 (*History of U.S. Decision-making Process on Vietnam Policy*). It had been commissioned in 1967 by the then Secretary of Defense, Robert McNamara. These papers had been prepared by a group of researchers, including Dr. Daniel Ellsberg, who "leaked" the secret documents to the press, and were based on Defense, CIA, and other secret files. Ellsberg said that he had once been a "hawk" on the Vietnamese war but had been converted to a "dove"; that American global interests could not justify the death of thousands of civilians in Southeast Asia; that the war now repelled him morally; and that he was prepared to take the consequences for his efforts to end U.S. involvement in Vietnam. Ellsberg and his companion Anthony Russo were arrested and charged with the theft of government property and unauthorized possession of national defense documents.

When the *Times* refused the request of the Attorney-general to cease publication of the papers, the government sought an injunction against it and other newspapers on the ground that their publication endangered national security. The case quickly reached the Supreme Court on appeal. By the end of June 1971, a sharply divided Court (all nine justices wrote separate opinions) held that the government did not have the inherent powers to "prior restraint"—that is, to prevent the publication of the papers—or that the injury done by publication could outweigh the constitutional guarantees of the freedom of the press. Justice Douglas asserted that, "Open debate and discussion of public issues are vital to our national health." Chief Justice Burger, along with Justices Blackmun and Harlan in dissent, said that the Court had insufficient time to weigh the important issues

UPI PHOTO

Members of the U.S. Supreme Court are shown here in a 1970 formal group portrait. The Justices are left to right, front row, Associate Justice John Harlan, Associate Justice Hugo L. Black, Chief Justice Warren E. Burger, Associate Justice William O. Douglas, and Associate Justice William J. Brennan, Jr.; back row, Associate Justice Thurgood Marshall, Associate Justice Potter Stewart, Associate Justice Byron R. White, and Associate Justice Harry A. Blackmun.

in the case and determine whether the publication would have the serious effects on the war and international relations alleged by the government. Nevertheless, the majority did not imply that the guarantees of free press in the First Amendment gave newspapers an absolute right to publish anything under all circumstances, nor that persons involved in the disclosures were immune to criminal prosecution.

The case involved basic issues—freedom of the press and the right of the people to know, versus the right of the same public through its spokesman, the President or persons delegated by him, to have its foreign business transacted in a responsible and confidential manner. It also raised the issue of the ethics of former or present government officials who divulge confidential documents that they were pledged to respect. On the other hand, some charged that too many of the papers had been labeled secret that really could be published without damaging the national interest. Some others worried about the precedent set by the publication of the Pentagon Papers, fearing that it might impair the ability of the government to negotiate with other powers privately and in confidence without a possibility of premature disclosure.

The Pentagon Papers controversy also reopened the debate on the merits of the Vietnam war. Opponents of the war charged that President Johnson had been false to his pledge during the 1964 presidential campaign that he did not seek a wider war and that "American boys should not be sent to fight a war that Asian boys should be fighting"; and they charged also that he had planned the bombing of North Vietnam and the sending of troops into combat. They professed to have evidence from the papers that Americans were duped by the government in the matter of alleged attacks on U.S. vessels by North Vietnamese forces in the Gulf of Tonkin in 1964. In reality, they said, previous attacks on North Vietnam by South Vietnamese ships and U.S. planes had brought on the incident. Casualties from bombing raids, it was claimed, were sometimes 80 percent civilian.

Defenders of American policy (including Nixon officials who were forced into the position of defending the war policy of the Johnson Administration) observed that the disclosures did not cite the actions of the North Vietnamese in moving their regular army into South Vietnam and thereby changing the strategic picture in Southeast Asia. The Pentagon Papers showed, they continued, that American leaders had carefully considered the impact of the war on Southeast Asia and on American interests and had agonized over the hard but necessary decisions; that the problems in getting out of Vietnam were immense; that when the U.S. government had ordered in the troops, it was convinced that North Vietnam threatened the security of all Southeast Asia; and that the government had underestimated the persistence and determination of the Vietcong and North Vietnamese. In commenting on U.S. motives in entering the war, Secretary of State Rusk said that the country had acted on a notion of collective security, that is, it had sought to avoid World War III by honoring its SEATO treaty commitments to Southeast Asia peoples of Laos, South Vietnam, and Cambodia. He admitted that the strategic idea which had been viable for a generation was losing force. "My generation has become old and tired," Rusk said, "and it doesn't grip us in the way it used to when I was young. Half of our people are so young they had had no chance to live through or to remember these experiences, so it is understandable that it doesn't grip them in the same way."

Some observers neither in favor nor against the war were amazed at some of the revelations concerning U.S. diplomacy, as, for example, the events surrounding the overthrow and assassination in November 1963 of the President of South Vietnam, Ngo Dinh Diem, and his brother. U.S. officials during the Kennedy administration "sanctioned and encouraged" the *coup d'état* against President Diem. During the progress of the *coup,* U.S. Ambassador Lodge cabled the State Department, "We are launched on a course from which there is no respectable turning back: the overthrow of the Diem Government." The ambassador who preceded Lodge, and who favored Diem, was convinced that the backing of the rebel generals by the U.S. government was a mistake because it saddled Americans with the obligation of propping up rebel leaders who were unable to govern South Vietnam and therefore made it possible for the Vietcong to endanger the country.

Critics sneered at intellectuals like Ellsberg who now lamented the war which they had helped to justify when they were part of the Kennedy and Johnson Administrations. Such men were inclined to forget that the conflict had been an "intellectual's war" in its origin. Now that it had become unpopular, said their critics, they wanted to disassociate themselves from it and regain political power. Regardless of the arguments, it was clear that anger and distrust of U.S. policy at home and abroad further eroded support of the war. It was commonplace to hear charges that the United States deliberately escalated and widened the scope of the war in the 1960's and in the process misled the Congress and American people.

CIVIL RIGHTS AND MINORITIES

In the trial of the "Chicago Seven," mentioned in last year's *Record,* Judge Julius J. Hoffman sentenced four defendants and their principal defense attorneys, William M. Kunstler and Leonard I. Weinglass, to jail terms ranging from eight months to over four years for their flagrant contempt of court. The liberal press assailed the judge for the severe sentences, while many "law and order" adherents applauded his action. The jury acquitted all seven of conspiracy to incite riot during the Democratic National Convention of 1968, but found five guilty of individual acts of inciting to riot. Bobby Seale, originally indicted with the "Seven" had his case severed from the rest. Judge Hoffman sentenced him to three months' imprisonment on each of sixteen counts of contempt of court because his behavior in court had been "contumacious." Some legal observers called the sentence the longest for criminal contempt in the history of Anglo-American jurisprudence.

Civil libertarians followed with alarm the efforts of the government in January 1971 to indict in Harrisburg, Pennsylvania, six persons on charges of conspiracy to kidnap presidential adviser Henry A. Kissinger, for the purpose of holding him hostage until the Vietnamese War was ended and political prisoners were set free. The defendants were also charged with conspiring to blow up the heating systems of some government buildings in Washington. The accused dubbed the "Harrisburg Six," were Catholic radical peace activists. They included Reverend Philip F. Berrigan, already in prison for his part in the illegal acts of the "Catonsville Nine," another priest, an ex-priest, and a nun. Among the alleged co-conspirators was Berrigan's priest-brother, Daniel.

Generally speaking, a decline occurred in black militancy from its peaks in 1968 and 1969. Pressure and protest continued, however, over the remaining goals of the Civil Rights Movement in the areas of economic and political gains, as opposed to strictly legal rights. The decline in militancy reflected a change in tactics from political protest to consolidation of economic gains made by blacks in the 1960's. Blacks, who formed about eleven percent of the U.S. population in 1970, improved their lot, although their gains did not bring them parity with whites. The median income of all nonwhite families doubled in the 1960's and many climbed out of poverty. Other gains were a measure of their economic progress: a reduction in illiteracy; an increase in the number of black youths attending and graduating from college; and an increase in their proportionate numbers in professional and technical positions. But the progress was disappointing to many because they observed that, while educated blacks did make long strides, poor blacks failed to keep pace with either their black or white fellow citizens. Their unemployment rate was nearly double that of whites. Possibly, a wide gulf might yet divide poor blacks from both middle class blacks and whites.

Many black people charged that laws, court decisions, and the sundry local, State, and national rules of the 1960's had failed to achieve their goals because the government had not enforced them. Lack of money, personnel, and loss of will, they maintained, undermined the enforcement effort. This discontent received support in a report of the U.S. Commission on Human Rights, headed by the Reverend Theodore M. Hessburgh of Notre Dame University, which was released on October 12, 1970. Although the lengthy report acknowledged progress in desegregating public facilities and places of public accommodation, in insuring voting rights in Southern states and in increasing the percentage of black children attending integrated schools there, it held that there had been a major breakdown in the enforcement of existing legislation against racial discrimination. It lamented the fact that a substantial majority of black children still attended segregated schools, that extensive school segregation existed in the North and West, and that progress was poor in providing equal employment and housing opportunities to blacks. It characterized the government's enforcement of civil rights as "poorly coordinated and unfocused" and exhorted the President to be a courageous moral leader and end the failure to enforce existing laws, a charge it also leveled at his predecessors. Attacks on the Nixon Administration's record were similarly made by the Director of the

Office for Civil Rights in HEW, Leon E. Panetta, who resigned in protest.

The Nixon Administration asserted, however, that many black leaders with close ties to the Democratic Party had ignored its achievements for partisan reasons. It pointed with pride to the appointment of blacks to top government positions; to the naming of eleven blacks to the Federal bench; to the increase in the civil-rights budget of HEW; to more school desegregation in the South in two years than in the preceding fifteen; to the promotion of fair housing; and to its Philadelphia Plan to integrate the building trades.

Blacks maintained on the other hand that the Nixon Administration was hostile to their interests and aspirations. They contended that its emphasis on law and order encouraged police and local officials to deal sternly with civil rights protestors, and that its effort to economize had the effect of reducing funds for black-related projects. Its "Southern strategy" favored whites over blacks, and its interest in Republican suburbs meant the neglect of inner cities with minority residents. That the Nixon Administration was not disposed to sponsor additional civil rights legislation was clear to all. In February 1970, Dr. Daniel Patrick Moynihan, a presidential aide, wrote a memorandum suggesting that the time may have come when the issue of race could benefit from a period of "benign neglect."

The problem of segregation of the schools was difficult to solve without arousing deep emotion on all sides. Seeking to end or preserve it produced political storms not easy to calm. The continuing steps of the Federal government to desegregate schools were controversial. A particular target of the government was *de facto* racial segregation in the schools and in housing in the suburbs and Northern cities. HEW threatened some Northern cities with the loss of Federal aid if their schools discriminated against blacks; the Department of Justice filed lawsuits calling for an end to racial discrimination; and the Department of Housing and Urban Development pressured local authorities to plan low-cost housing if they wanted money for urban renewal, water, sewage, and other projects.

Negroes continued to migrate to the big cities. In 1970, 53 percent remained in the South, as opposed to 77 percent thirty years before. The migration brought black majorities to Washington, D.C.; Newark, New Jersey; Atlanta, Georgia; and Gary, Indiana, and sizeable minorities in other localities. The black vote became more important to the political parties, for it could no longer be taken for granted by the Democrats. As Representative Shirley Chisholm of New York, a leader in the Civil Rights Movement, said, "Blacks are fed up with Democrats as with the Republicans—many think the Democrats have taken the blacks for granted too long."

With growing frequency blacks received appointments to positions of prestige and influence. Samuel Lee Gravely, Jr., became the first black admiral in the U.S. Navy (1971). An increase in the number of appointed and elected officials who were black was testimony to their growing influence. In June 1970, Kenneth Gibson, an engineer, won the mayoralty in Newark. The campaign waged for so many years, to register black voters and to educate them politically showed impressive results. In the 92nd Congress, twelve black Representatives (a net gain of three)—all Democrats—and Senator Edward W. Brooke (Republican of Massachusetts) formed the Black Caucus for the purpose of maintaining a "swing position," that is, the ability to provide votes needed to pass bills they favored and to block measures they deemed inimical to the interests of their race.

In the off-year elections in 1971, the success of black candidates did not meet expectations. Charles Evers failed badly in his effort to become Governor of Mississippi, while Arnold R. Pinkney lost his bid to succeed Carl B. Stokes as Mayor of Cleveland.

The most effective instrument for advancing rights for blacks and integration was the Supreme Court. It held in *Griggs v. Duke Power Company* (1971) that the Civil Rights Act of 1964 prohibited requirements such as a high-school diploma and certain scores on intelligence tests, unless they were necessary for the satisfactory performance of a job. The Court determined that the power company had used these requirements to discriminate against blacks. In January 1970, it ruled that school districts in six deep-South states had to integrate before February 1. The deadline passed with little effect, because public school officials were planning further legal skirmishes in the courts.

In April 1971, the Court unanimously ordered the end of dual school systems (separate schools for white and black children) and upheld busing for reasonable distances as a proper means of achieving racial balance. But

UPI PHOTO

Mrs. Bella Abzug, center, and Mrs. Shirley Chisholm, second from right, women members of Congress, announcing June, 1971, that they have asked for a meeting with President Nixon to discuss issues of concern to women. With them are representatives of women's groups in Massachusetts.

it left it to lower courts to pass on specific busing proposals. It said that objection to busing "may have validity when the time or distance of travel is so great as to risk either the health of the children or significantly impinge on the educational process." It declared unconstitutional antibusing laws passed by North Carolina and New York. But in October 1971, the Supreme Court declined to hear an appeal by the Pontiac, Michigan school board of a court-ordered busing plan. Pontiac was the scene of violence, including the burning of school buses. The Court did not pass on the question of segregation in the schools resulting from housing patterns as contrasted with a deliberate segregation policy.

Prospects of confrontations between white and black parents worried politicians. White parents were especially vehement against busing their children outside their own neighborhoods to schools they regarded as either unsafe or inferior. Formation in some areas of antibusing organizations heightened the angry mood of many Americans. Some black parents opposed having their children bused outside their own area and thereby deprived of the opportunity to develop pride in "blackness" which was emphasized in largely black schools.

In Richmond, Virginia, an order was handed down to school officials by U.S. Judge Robert E. Merhige, Jr., requiring them to bus some 25,000 out of a total of 48,500 pupils in September 1971. Bitter protests culminated in threats on the judge's life and the need to provide him with armed guards. Public resentment against Federal demands for massive busing now welled up. It was directed at a variety of court or HEW orders that would have meant the busing of about 300,000 children before the opening of the school year in September 1971. The widespread and vocal opposition from the affected localities was a signal that plans for desegregation would encounter a series of political obstacles before they could be implemented. The Nixon Administration had to make a choice which would certainly arouse the antagonism of one group or another in the highly polarized situation. The President chose a policy of minimum busing. He would enforce the law against racially separate schools but would oppose busing if it were done for the purpose of achieving racial balance. Accordingly, he ordered Federal officials to hold such busing to a minimum and he promised to aid school districts with their problems of segregation. This policy did not prevent the government from filling suits against a number of Southern school districts to speed up desegregation. Later, the Administration sought to delay court-ordered busing plans in a move to appease public opinion. All in all, however, segregation in Southern schools dropped significantly in 1970–1971.

Some political leaders were more vocal in their opposition to busing. Governor George Wallace of Alabama, who wanted to be nominated by the Democrats for the Presidency in 1972, won wide support for his attacks on busing and he issued three executive orders instructing state school boards to ignore desegregation plans approved by the courts. "I have nothing but utter contempt for the courts of the land." Politicians recognized busing as a potentially explosive issue in the electoral campaign of 1972.

In February 1970, Congress approved educational appropriations bills that were amended to express its opposition to busing of children for the purpose of achieving desegregation. The bill signed by the President in July 1971 forbade the use of funds to compel more desegregation. Strong sentiment in the Congress against busing also surfaced in the debates over the President's proposals for higher education. In November 1971, in an amendment to the Higher Education Bill, the House voted in favor of prohibiting the use of Federal funds for busing, restraining Federal officials from encouraging local authorities to use local funds for busing, and stipulating that no Federal court order requiring busing be effective until all appeals had been exhausted. The Senate adopted a milder attitude which tried to curb busing without interfering with desegregation.

Indifference and hostility to some of the goals of the Civil Rights Movement dictated a change in direction in the drive to secure rights and benefits for blacks. Since demonstrations, boycotts, and marches seemed less effective, organizations turned to economic and political goals. Their object was to employ economic and political leverage to get more and better jobs for black men and women. There was a widespread abandonment of the old goal of integration in favor of racial separation and black nationalism. The NAACP, however, persisted in its avowedly integrationist course.

Major organizations like NAACP, SCLC, and the Urban League still attracted much support in communities. But some newer groups challenged their desire to achieve progress by peaceful means. The most notable of the groups embracing violence as a technique to bring political and social change was the Black Panther Party, established in 1966. Their slogan was "Black Power" and their object the undertaking of a socialist revolution in accordance with the ideas of Malcolm X and inspired by Mao Tse-tung, Che Guevara, and Regis Debray. The bulk of American blacks refused to support the Panthers, though it sympathized with their efforts to help.

The Black Power groups splintered and disagreed. In February 1971, the Panthers expelled Eldridge Cleaver for "counterrevolutionary" activities. He in turn expelled Huey Newton, who asserted that the party would not use violence but instead would work within the existing political system.

Attempts of various State and local authorities to prosecute the Panthers were generally unsuccessful. In New Haven, Connecticut, in 1971, Ericka Huggins and Bobby Seale were freed of charges of murder and kidnapping when the jury was unable to reach a verdict. In New York City, thirteen Panthers charged with conspiracy to bomb police stations and public buildings, with attempted murder of policemen, with arson, and with concealing weapons, were not convicted. After his first conviction was reversed by an appeals court, Huey Newton was tried again on charges of voluntary manslaughter of a policeman in 1967 in Oakland, California. In 1971 a jury could not agree on a verdict.

Hot controversy raged over a police raid on the Black Panthers in Chicago which had taken place in December 1969. A grand jury in that city in June 1971 brought charges against the State Attorney of Illinois and other officials in connection with the shooting during the raid of Panther leaders Fred Hampton and Mark Clark.

Attention in the black militant movement centered on Angela Davis, a young philosophy instructor at the University of California, and a self-avowed Communist revolutionary. She got even more notoriety after being charged with murder. In 1970, during a trial at the Marin County Courthouse in San Raphael, California, a spectator, Jonathan Jackson, passed guns to the defendant who was on trial for stabbing two black convict witnesses. Jackson took as hostages the judge, Harold J. Haley, the prosecuting attorney, and three woman jurors. A gunfight followed in the parking lot where the judge, two convicts, and Jackson were slain, while the district attorney and a juror were seriously wounded. A warrant was issued for Angela Davis' arrest, charging that she had bought the guns used in the kidnapping and murders and had conspired with Jackson. She had been interested in the "Soledad brothers" case which concerned three black convicts accused of killing a Soledad Prison guard. One of the convicts was George Jackson, brother of Jonathan and lover of Angela Davis. George Jackson was killed during an attempted escape in August 1971.

Angela Davis disappeared but was captured in New York City by the FBI. Her case attracted international interest. For many her trial and imprisonment inspired the sort of fervor that had been common to professed liberals during the Sacco-Vanzetti and the Rosenberg trials. She cut a romantic figure as a young, beautiful woman, a black radical, an intellectual fighting injustice and intolerance, and a lover. But many others saw her instead as a "knee-jerk" Communist quite prepared to commit any enormity on behalf of the revolution.

Since a large percentage of persons in jail were black, the issue of "prisoner rights" was of particular concern to Afro-Americans. Much publicity was given by the press and television to deplorable prison conditions, the rights of prisoners, the plans of reformers and militants, and especially to speculation on the causes of prison riots. Within the prisons, blacks and Puerto Ricans were politicized by militants, notably the Panthers, who took credit for what they called the "Prison Movement" whose goal was the protection and liberation of political prisoners and the convict class in general. Men behind bars are understandably receptive to the idea that prisoners are victims of a racist society and that in effect they are political prisoners and not criminals. The militants mounted a campaign to secure a ban against prison brutality, freedom to communicate freely with lawyers, and the rights to secure adequate medical care, to correspond, and even to vote in all elections.

The general social atmosphere was conducive to the "Prison Movement." In some circles, the conviction was strong that criminal conduct was only one part of a complex social problem and that the offender was really not morally culpable. Instead, society at large was to blame. The general air of permissiveness tended to blur the outlines of personal responsibility for behavior. The dizzy speed of social change in the world beyond prison walls naturally had its effect on inmates—now aided by "civil rights attorneys"—to demand rights and pursue appeals to the highest courts. A growing number of civilian volunteers furnished all sorts of services to prison inmates. Organizations of ex-offenders furnished advice and help to prisoners who were paroled or had completed their sentences. Through personal appearances and publicity, they encouraged a more tolerant attitude toward those still in prison and swelled the flood of sentiment for reform of the prisons.

Outbursts occurred in a number of State and Federal prisons. The bloodiest incident was at the State Correctional Facility in Attica, New York, where on September 9, 1971, the inmates rebelled, held thirty-eight guards as hostages, and threatened them with death if their demands were not met. Among the demands were complete amnesty from criminal prosecution and transportation to a "non-imperialist" country. Governor Nelson Rockefeller ordered State troopers and police to storm the Attica prison on September 13th when negotiations seemed to falter. In the ensuing fight, eleven guards and employees and thirty-two inmates died or were fatally wounded.

The Attica riot became a topic of controversy from the outset. Among the questions raised were: should outside negotiators like Black Panther Bobby Seale and radical attorney William Kunstler have been brought in as mediators? Would more negotiations with the prisoners have produced a solution without bloodshed? Should Rockefeller have met with the prisoners? Was the riot premeditated and the work of militants? Is society safe if the authorities bargain with convicted felons? The Governor stoutly maintained that the rebellion was due to the "highly organized revolutionary tactics of militants" and to outside forces. On the other hand, the Black Panthers justified the takeover as "a human response to the violence and suffering the brothers had long endured."

Conflicting testimony was given about how the hostages had died and about the measures necessary to quell the riot. A year later, a commission appointed by Rockefeller reported that the outbreak was spontaneous and that he ought to have talked with the prisoners. The report only sharpened the controversy. Throughout the State and the nation, popular opinion held that judges and reformers were too soft on prisoners and were thereby contributing to the staggering problems that faced prison guards and officials. Riots which occurred in other parts of the country rendered the problem of prisons an immediate and pressing subject, which had no easy solutions.

Increasing governmental and private attention focused on the American Indians in 1970 and 1971. Although they formed less than half of one percent of the population, the complaints of Indians were now heard and the "centuries of injustice" and neglect accorded them were lamented on every side. An example of the changed attitude toward them was found in the pages of Dee Brown's *Bury My Heart at Wounded Knee* which retold the loss of the West to the white man. In July 1970, President Nixon sent a message to Congress on the condition of the Indians whom he described as "the first Americans" and as "the most deprived and most isolated minority group in our nation." His proposed remedies included the end of the policy of terminating Indian tribes (the forced ending of trusteeship over Indian communities by the Federal Government). Forced ending would have practical consequences of disorientation, and a worsening of the economic and social conditions of many Indians. The President urged more self-government, and Indian control of Federal programs aimed at aiding the reservations. He also called for improvement in schooling; more money for economic development and health programs; and the assignment of a special Under Secretary in the Department of the Interior to handle Indian problems. The Nixon Administration was embarrassed by conflict among officials and the contrast between the noble intentions expressed by the President and recommendations to assist the Indians made by the Interior Department officers. The example of militants in the black and other minority communities was not lost on Indian activists who applied the tactics of the Civil Rights Movement, litigation and violent confrontation. They occupied certain sites, including Alcatraz in San Francisco Bay in November 1969, as a way of dramatizing their cause.

EDUCATION AND YOUTH PROBLEMS

Many of the nation's high schools experienced a marked increase in disruptions and violence, including teacher or student strikes, fire, vandalism, riots, and physical attacks on both teachers and students. Some of these incidents were related to racial tensions. The police had to be called in to quell disturbances either in the corridors and classrooms or in the buses carrying boys and girls to and from their classes.

Bombings, acts of arson or attempted arson occurred on college campuses. In the 1969–1970 academic year there were nearly 1800 student demonstrations, sit-ins, arsons, and building seizures and about 7500 arrests. Late in February 1970 violence erupted for several days around the University of California campus at Santa Barbara, and about a week later a town house in Greenwich Village in New York City was destroyed, probably as a result of an accidental explosion touched off by young radicals assembling devices in a "bomb factory."

Following the invasion of Cambodia by American and South Vietnamese forces, demonstrations and protests erupted throughout the land and especially on college campuses. On May 4, 1970 four young people were shot to death on the campus of Kent State University, Ohio, by National Guardsmen who were quelling student disorders that had gripped the school for months.

The dissatisfaction of black students intensified as a result of a clash between police and students at Jackson State College, Mississippi, on May 15, 1970, when two young blacks were killed. This tragedy followed close on the heels of the blacks shot by police during a riot in Atlanta, Georgia on May 11th. President Nixon met with the heads of fifteen black colleges in order to seek ways of easing tension on campuses; and Dr. Ralph Abernathy led a 100-mile march through Georgia's black belt ending at Atlanta to protest the growing repression of blacks and students.

The American incursion into Cambodia and the shootings of students at Kent State enraged antiwar and other students. Normal campus life was at an end. Classes and final examinations were canceled on many campuses to enable students to devote all their energies to protest and to carry their message to the people.

On August 24, 1970 a tremendous explosion destroyed the Army Mathematics Research Center at the University of Wisconsin, killing a physicist. The FBI accused three young men of sabotage, conspiracy, and of conspiracy to destroy government property. The state of Wisconsin indicted them for murder and arson. The disorders and threats of violence led to the adoption of preventive measures like more campus guards, and identification cards for students and instructors. The President of the United States requested Congress to grant the FBI authority to enter campus disorders without waiting to be summoned by local authorities.

The sad events at Kent State and Jackson State College occasioned the appointment of a presidential commission on campus unrest headed by former Governor William W. Scranton of Pennsylvania. The Scranton Report condemned not only youthful terrorists and permissive college officials, but police and politicians who overreacted to protests, and urged the President to exert moral leadership toward the goal of reconciliation of all elements in the nation. In its view, campus protests were directed to the war in Southeast Asia, civil liberties, and reform of the universities whose goals and structures were opposed by the protestors. On the other hand, a grand jury at Kent, Ohio, indicted 25 persons, including the president of the student body and a member of the Sociology Department, but excluding National Guardsmen. It blamed the university administration for

WIDE WORLD PHOTO

Kent State University in Ohio was the scene of disorders on May 5, 1970, following the shooting of four persons the day before. The shooting took place behind the building at upper left. National Guardsmen are seen lined up in the center of the campus. In the foreground is the burned out ROTC building, previously destroyed by students in protest of the U.S. invasion of Cambodia.

fostering "an attitude of laxity, overindulgence, and permissiveness," some instructors for a disproportionate emphasis on dissent, and finally the students for bad behavior.

The campus revolutionaries were seized by the idea
that the college or university was a model of society at
large and that, therefore, their victories at school were a
prelude to greater victories in the battle against the "establishment." The schools were responsible in some measure for their troubles. They admitted thousands of students who had neither the capacity nor the commitment
to the objectives of a liberal and a scientific training; they
encouraged them to entertain an inflated notion about
their abilities and noble intentions; they held up academic training as a social and personal panacea; they encouraged students to take moral stands on a variety of
public questions without the competence to pass moral
judgment based on ethical and religious foundations;
and they convinced too many that it is possible to solve
all problems humanely by employing technological and
scientific means.

In colleges and universities throughout the land rising
costs and inadequate funds led to hard times. The re-
trenchment was especially trying for private institutions
which found it increasingly difficult to compete with the
large municipal or state colleges that charged little or no
tuition. Perhaps the root cause of the financial plight of
the schools was a decline in public confidence in the
mission of higher education and more particularly in the
liberal arts. Many Americans were apparently unwilling

to bear the heavy burdens to support instructors and staff and to enlarge facilities so that enrollments could rise.

The young were not the only ones convinced of their moral superiority and their benevolent role in reforming America and the world. Some of their most enthusiastic supporters were their elders. Charles A. Reich, a forty-two-year-old professor at Yale University Law School, spoke glowingly of them in his *The Greening of America* with the theme that young people were already shaping tomorrow and that their behavior condemned as irrational, immoral, or antisocial by the establishment was the only means they could employ to create a new and humane society. The revolution of the new generation could have its ultimate creation, Reich asserted, as a higher reason, a more human community, and a new and liberated individual. One of Reich's terms, "Consciousness III," was felt by a few individuals in the 1960's but soon was used widely and spread to many. It was a product of the promise of life made to young Americans by affluence, technology, liberation, ideals and by the threat to the promise of "neon ugliness, boring jobs, and the war in Vietnam." The new consciousness found expression in the informal mode of dress and especially in the new music, it filled young people with the power to transcend obstacles and with a childlike, breathless sense of wonder; and it impelled them to be socially concerned and to reject authority or work that was boring or irrelevant.

There is little doubt that young people were preoccupied with getting rid of pollution and returning to nature. They were repelled by modern science and technology, which had enjoyed their heyday in the 1950's and 1960's. Some advocated transforming consciousness to return the human race to the period before modern technology. The paradox was that these same enthusiasts would find it impossible to forego their amplifiers, electric guitars, stereo rigs, drugs, motorcycles, and modern highways which they used to thumb rides and be mobile —all products of an advanced technology.

Aware of their place in society and confident of their analysis of what was wrong, many youths asserted themselves within their families, the classrooms, and the public forum as perhaps no other generation in history. Americans were scarcely surprised to read that, during a White House ceremony on December 3, 1970, a nineteen-year-old woman who was receiving a Young American Medal for Public Service told the startled President, "I find it hard to believe in your sincerity in giving the awards until you get us out of Vietnam."

The youth revolt of the 1960's died down. Although some students retained an attachment to radical causes, they were not prepared to protest as vigorously as they had a few years before, and their elders were not prepared to regard them with ill-concealed amusement. The causes of the decline were many. The usual letdown following emotionally charged campaigns, and weariness both on the part of the young, who were drained of their energies, and on the part of the old, who had had enough, partly explained the decline. A major source of youthful discontent was removed in the "winding down" of the war in Vietnam. With a large segment of the American public and the government committed to ending hostilities, the youthful protesters could complain now only about the speed of the military withdrawal from Southeast Asia. Moreover, the excesses of some revolutionaries in bombing and other acts of violence seemed to belie their noble aspirations for a world of peace, love, and brotherhood. The sordidness of life among colonies of young people in New York, San Francisco, and other big cities, the bad "trips" experienced by those who took overdoses of hard drugs, the increase in venereal disease accompanying the new sexual freedom, and the greed which supposedly did not exist among the young and the innocent all furnished evidence that the reality of the world was removed from the youths' great expectations. It was as hard to reconcile with utopia the motorcycle gangs and criminal elements who used the cover of a youthful way of life to bring violence to some colonies, as it was to behold in the communes the same conflicting tensions (the interests of the whole versus the urges of members "to do their own thing" in the matter of sex and household chores) that were condemned when they appeared in "corrupt, American society." A symbol of the state of the youthful colonies was the Haight-Asbury district in the city of San Francisco which became a scene of desolation and despair, not of buoyant hope and optimism as it had been in the mid-sixties.

The causes of the decline were not all within the youth movement itself. The "establishment" was prepared for new onslaughts and was scarcely disposed to concede readily to youthful demands. The killing of four students at Kent State University during demonstrations had an inhibiting effect on radical students, as had the march of construction workers who broke up an antiwar rally in the Wall Street area on May 8, 1970, and the mass arrests made by Washington, D.C. police of protestors bent on grinding the government to a halt. Here and there a stiffening of attitude toward the young was noticeable. The town fathers of Middlefield, Connecticut, for example, barred in the courts a three-day rock festival at the Powder Ridge ski area planned for July 1970 on the grounds that it would be a public nuisance. A large group, cut off from local residents by police, did spend a weekend there which was described in the press as "drugs, sex, and nudity."

Television, which fanned the flames of student protest by giving it a national platform, prepared the way for its eventual failure by bringing into the American living room scenes of youthful disruption that alarmed viewers. Legislators were reluctant to appropriate vast sums to maintain and expand the activities of public colleges and universities which they associated with the "rebellion" of students and professors in the 1960's; they were less indulgent toward the young, so that when faced with the necessity of cutting expenditures because of the economic crisis confronting the nation as a whole, they achieved a double purpose in turning down expanded school budgets and teaching the academic world a lesson. In the huge appropriations bill for the Office of Education signed in July 1971 there was a provision that denied funds to anyone in a college or university who had been involved in forceful acts or threats of force in campus disturbances since August 1, 1969. Furthermore, the troubled state of the economy led to a smaller demand for college grad-

UPI PHOTO

Earth Day was observed April, 1970 by many young people, emphasizing the growing interest in ecology. Attention was drawn to the many ways in which our natural environment was being endangered. Here students paddle up the Milwaukee River in odd-looking craft to protest the polluted water.

uates who found that they were no longer eagerly pursued by corporations or government bureaus to recruit them.

Youthful energies were channelled in directions other than violent protest. For example, the young along with conservationists observed April 22, 1970, as Earth Day. Another interesting phenomenon was the Jesus People movement in which thousands of young men and women turned to Jesus Christ as personal saviour, to strict personal morality, to Bible reading, and to "speaking in tongues." This movement resembled the revivalism of earlier times. The rock musical *Jesus Christ Superstar,* while by no means part of the movement, nevertheless showed how timely religion was for the young. How lasting an attraction the movement would have for the young was a topic of discussion among clerics and sociologists. Still other young people were attracted to various Pentecostal sects within the Protestant and Catholic churches which emphasized a highly personal and emotional religious experience.

Another channel was "establishment politics," that is, participation in the campaigns and affairs of Republican and Democratic parties, especially in their so called reform wings. Some youths, mindful of the failure of protest politics, decided to "work within the system" to effect the changes they sought in society. Many volunteered their services to assist the underprivileged in the slums. A number of political leaders deliberately courted the youth vote and young activists to assist in local, State, and national campaigns. Some young people were attracted by the activities of Ralph Nader, a consumer's advocate, who organized task forces of young people to investigate the quality of consumer products and services, as well as the operation of government.

How many young people "dropped out" is unknown. It seemed that a minority gave themselves to a twilight existence of drugs or alcohol, to the trappings of oriental mysticism, to aimless travel in an effort to "find" themselves, or to join rural communes based on brotherly love and harmony. Dropping out was made possible by the fact that their subsistence was guaranteed by the society, parents and elders, who for the very reason they provided the material means were even more hated. What George Orwell said of the writers of the 1920's might be said of the dropouts who received assistance from parents or from public welfare, "People with empty bellies never despair of the universe, nor even think about it, for that matter." A strong current in youth groups was the disillusionment that follows activity and the failure of utopian dreams. There was a conviction that the world was worse than it is—colder, grayer, harder.

Americans have always had a love of youth. Ogden Nash, who died in 1971, wrote about turning thirty:*

> I kicked, I scratched, I bit my nails,
> I indulged in tantrums the size of whales,
> I found it hard to forgive my mater
> For not having had me ten years later.

The youth movement gave new importance to the

* "Lines to be Scribbled on Somebody Else's Thirtieth Milestone," in *Verses from 1929 On*. Copyright © 1934 by Ogden Nash. Quoted by permission of Little, Brown and Co.

necessity of "staying young" which had a certain am-
bience of innocence, idealism, and self-sacrifice. Despite
private misgivings, Americans ritually acknowledged the
merits and virtues of their young (a term that encom-
passed sons and daughters in their twenties and even in
their thirties). The adoption of the 26th Amendment to
the Constitution giving eighteen-year-olds the right to
vote appeared only proper and inevitable. The resolution
of the proposed amendment cleared Congress on March
23, 1971, was submitted to the States and was approved
in the record time of only three months and seven days.
The youth vote, first cast in the off-year elections on
November 2, 1971, did not apparently affect results in
major cities but it did in smaller cities and towns with
large universities. Some teenagers won elective office in
small towns and villages.

If imitation is the sincerest form of flattery, many older
Americans reflected their opinions by wearing long hair.
(Even former President Johnson who was forced out of
office partly because of youthful protest against his foreign policies, let his hair grow long and dignified law-
makers, who fulminated against the militancy of the
young, sported long sideburns in an effort to join the
"now generation.") The youthful style of informal fashion deeply affected how many Americans of all economic
levels dressed.

How permanent the cult of the young will be re-
mains to be seen. It may have been an oddity of the sixties
and a temporary sign of the strains caused by self-indul-
gence, too great an attachment to materialism, an aliena-
tion from traditional morality and values, and the loss of

faith in the ability of Americans to resolve their differences without violence, and indeed a loss of faith in the meaning of life itself.

THE WOMEN'S LIBERATION PROTEST

A source of considerable dissatisfaction with life for many American women was their own place or status. They were convinced that the 106 million women in the nation did not enjoy the proper rewards of their labor and contribution, particularly that the 30.8 million women (1970) who constituted over 40 percent of the work force were "second-class citizens" and were relatively scarce in professional or skilled positions. They were disappointed in the lack of progress in women's rights following the ratification of the 19th Amendment. The promise of progress which appeared bright in the 1920's and 1930's was unfulfilled, they charged; and although women had the vote and went to college in large numbers, few had achieved the highest elective or appointive offices. The better education of women in the 20th century ought to have entitled them to more lucrative and rewarding positions. Instead women's horizons had been limited to home and children although only a small part of their lives was now absorbed in the rearing of children or running a household.

There was clear evidence that women had moved into jobs that were once the domain of men. Federal regulations accorded antidiscrimination protection to women and private employers made some efforts to fill important positions with them. Furthermore the Equal Em-

ployment Opportunities Commission ruled that all jobs
must be offered to both men and women unless "sex is
a bona fide occupational qualification reasonably necessary to the normal operation" of a particular business.
The Civil Rights Act of 1964 also aided the women's
cause by banning sex discrimination in employment. The
first women's rights case to come before the Supreme
Court under the Civil Rights Act was *Phillips v. Martin
Marietta Corp.,* in which the Court held that it was unlawful not to employ women with young children unless
the same prohibition applied to male applicants.

Despite the fact that the number of women holding
policy-making positions in the Federal government and
in private business rose sharply, many feminists charged
that only "token" concessions were being made to
women. They pointed to the findings of the President's
Commission on the Status of Women (1965) that wages
paid to women were discriminatory and that propor-
tionately fewer women were in the professions or on
executive levels. They charged that there was little ready
action to implement the Commission's recommendations, including child-care centers that would enable
mothers to be gainfully employed while their children
were supervised by others during business hours.

A militant movement developed to promote the welfare and progress of women. The New Feminism was
usually called "Women's Liberation" or "Women's Lib."
Some of its support came from civil rights advocates. Just
as abolitionists were supported by feminists in the 19th
century, so in the late 1960's and early 1970's civil rights
activists made common cause with women militants.

Other encouragement came from the antiwar protestors and dissenters who saw the "establishment" as the joint enemy of women and peace. Actually, the protest movements resulted from similar forces: the homogenization of society or the tendency to encourage uniformity in standards and behavior, the elimination of differences owing to religion, sex and race, the undermining of traditional standards of behavior and morality, the widespread American tendency to prize the right of each person "to do his own thing," and the vast publicity given to protest movements and colorful militants by the news media. Radio and television "talk-shows" regularly featured leading militants who carried their message to thousands across the land, and heralded the news of such progress as the opening of McSorley's Old Ale House to women (barred to them for over a century) and the appointment of girl pages for the first time in the history of the U.S. Senate.

The aspirations of many of the women militants could be studied in Betty Friedan's *The Feminine Mystique* (published in 1963). This title was her term for the difficult-to-define quality that inhibited women from asserting their rights and that left them feeling guilty when they did. Friedan maintained that it made women live lies and barred them from being full people in society. Women had to take themselves seriously as persons and help change society, she asserted.

"Women's libbers" wanted more than the homemaker-wife-mother role. They demanded independence. Some of their goals received general acceptance; equal pay for equal work, equal job opportunity, and equal treatment under the law. But other goals and charges were not well received: for example, their attacks on "male chauvinism," their feeling that women were merely "sex objects," or their demand that the "love, honor, and obey" phrase in the marriage ceremony be deleted. They objected to being called girls, ladies, Miss, or Mrs., and instead wanted to be called "Ms." They suggested that words like salesgirl and chairman be replaced by salesperson and chairperson.

Women's lib also affected religious bodies which sought to assign larger roles to women. The movement was not satisfied with token concessions; what it wanted was the recognition of women ministers, a step stoutly resisted by many congregations. Even the Roman Catholic Church felt the pressure. The activist Coalition of American Nuns opposed the governance of the church by all male bishops and Vatican officials.

On August 26, 1970, on the fiftieth anniversary of the 19th Amendment, a large demonstration called the Women's Strike for Equality March was held in New York City by women's liberation groups in order to dramatize the need for completing women's equality with men. The news media gave extensive coverage to the militants who locked arms and marched down Fifth Avenue in the company of some male supporters. Another highlight of the movement was the reading in Boston in March 1971 of a Declaration of Women's Independence. The women's lib groups agitated for the enactment of an Equal Rights Amendment to the Constitution which would recognize women as equal with men before the law. Some moderate women's groups raised

WIDE WORLD PHOTO
Demonstrators for women's rights marching in Rochester, New York, on their way to the home of Susan B. Anthony, the leading feminist at the turn of the century. The event celebrated the fiftieth anniversary of women's right to vote, won on August 26, 1920.

their voices against this proposal for fear that it might strip away from women certain beneficial protective laws.

The movement was a victim of competing groups of diverse philosophies and tactics. Among the largest were the National Organization for Women (NOW), established in 1966, and the National Women's Political Caucus. Some organizations sought legislation that would provide Federal support for a system of child-care centers and for free abortion-on-demand that would allow "woman to control her own body." They brought suits against certain State laws barring abortion. In 1970, their greatest victory occurred in the New York State legislature which permitted abortion within the first twenty-four weeks of pregnancy.

Some extreme theorists among women's libbers maintained that male and female sex roles would end with the overthrow of capitalism (which in their view was the source of competition between men and women and was the origin of private ownership of resources). A small minority advocated lesbianism and condemned marriage as a form of prostitution. The radical proposals hurt the movement. Many women rejected the extremists and noted that the differences between the sexes were not the result of institutions but were present in the Garden of Eden.

The "New Woman" in America was the subject of amusement among Europeans who regarded American women as the most pampered and indulged persons in the world. It was ironic that the New Feminism occurred in a land where women had already achieved what their sisters in most lands could only dream of. These observers saw as especially piquant the popularity among some American women of masculine characteristics: aggressiveness, the wearing of pants, and the like, which indicated that they were not agitating for women's rights but for the right to become men—that they were more anti-male than pro-female.

SPACE EXPLORATION AND TRANSPORTATION

In March 1970 the President set forth U.S. goals in space for the next decade, including sending unmanned spacecraft to all the planets in the solar system. Interest in space projects declined in both government and the public. How fickle public acclaim is and how quickly boredom sets in was demonstrated by the reaction to a successful moonlanding flight. Less than a year after the historic landing by Apollo 11, there was virtually no attention given to the lift-off, after some technical and medical difficulties, of the Apollo 13 from Cape Kennedy on April 11, 1970. The flight ran into trouble because of an explosion in the service module which occurred some 200,000 miles from earth. Disaster loomed ahead. But flight controllers on the ground devised certain maneuvers aimed at bringing home (on April 17th) astronauts James A. Lovell, Jr., Fred W. Haise, Jr., and John L. Swigert, Jr., who became objects of national worry until they landed safely. Other flights were postponed until changes in design could be made and thus avert a repetition of the near-calamity of Apollo 13.

Apollo 14, with Alan B. Shepard, Jr., Edgar D. Mitchell, and Stuart A. Roosa aboard, lifted off from Cape Kennedy at the end of January 1971 for another moonlanding. After some troubles in flight the astronauts touched down on the lunar surface in February in the Fra Mauro badlands. They explored the lunar surface, and set up scientific instruments and a nuclear generator.

On July 26, 1971, Apollo 15 took off in what was the longest and most complicated expedition to the moon. The crew headed by Colonel David R. Scott remained there for 67 hours, used a "dune buggy" (Lunar Roving Vehicle), a costly battery-powered car for lunar travel, collected rocks (including the "Genesis Rock," a crystalline rock that geologists said was as old as the moon itself), and conducted scientific and geological observations. The crew transmitted to earth color television pictures. The mission ended successfully on August 7th.

American efforts to learn more of the other planets succeeded. On May 30, 1971, the United States launched an unmanned spacecraft, Mariner 9, which orbited Mars after a five-and-a-half-month journey of 287,000,000 miles. Its purpose was to photograph the surface of Mars and of its two small moons, to map its terrain, and to gather data about its atmosphere. The Mariner's cameras recorded a raging "dust storm" and took pictures daily. In its search for evidence of life, it found considerable moisture at the poles, but as expected, no signs of life or of the legendary Martians. It sought sites for possible landings in the future. Astronomers were pleased by the vast body of information uncovered by Mariner 9. Unlike the Soviets who had made two space-probes of Mars, the U.S. announced some of its scientific findings.

These space accomplishments failed to convince Americans to support future missions with enthusiasm and financial support. Their interest was focused on national problems, not on the skies. As was expected by many the budget of NASA was pared, making it necessary to eliminate some Apollo flights. The budgetary cuts led to the laying off of thousands of highly skilled workers and scientists who joined the ranks of the unemployed in the "science depression" of 1970–1971.

The years 1970–1971 were difficult for airlines, which found it hard in the face of foreign competition to fill all seats on their expensive jumbo jets. But more vexing to Americans and foreigners alike was hijacking. For ideological and other reasons, some Americans hijacked planes and ordered them to Havana, Cuba. On August 2, 1970, for instance, a jumbo jet with 378 passengers and crew, flying from New York to Puerto Rico, was diverted to Cuba but was released. Most of the hijacks were of U.S. and Latin American planes. The Soviet Union did not escape, however, for in October 1970 a Russian plane was hijacked to Turkey.

The use of armed guards riding shotgun, as on the frontier with stagecoaches, proved effective. They inhibited some potential hijackers, as did the use of sophisticated devices to detect weapons on passengers or in their luggage.

Worldwide attention came on September 6, 1970, when two American and one Swiss airliners were hijacked in Europe by Arab commandoes of the Popular

Front for the Liberation of Palestine (PFLP). An attempted hijack of an Israeli plane failed. One of the American planes and the Swiss plane were flown to a desert airstrip in Jordan, where they were surrounded by guerrillas, who threatened to blow up the planes and their passengers if the Jordanian authorities intervened. The other American plane was flown to Cairo where it was blown up by the guerrillas after they had released the passengers and crew on September 7th. A British airliner was also hijacked later and joined the two in Jordan on the 9th. All three planes and over 300 passengers were held hostage to ransom seven Arab guerrillas being held in European jails. President Nixon called upon the international community "to take joint action to suspend airline services with those countries which refuse to punish or extradite hijackers involved in international blackmail"; the Secretary General of the United Nations, U Thant, deplored the air piracy; and the Security Council called on all the parties concerned to release at once all passengers and crews. Eventually on September 12th, after passengers and crews were let off, bombs placed on board by the guerrillas were detonated and the three planes were blown to pieces. The release of the hostages was made in exchange for the freeing of the jailed terrorists in European custody and the release of many Arabs detained in Israel.

A convention, the Suppression of Unlawful Seizure of Aircraft, was signed in December 1970 by representatives and observers of over seventy states, and went into effect in the following year. Despite this and other international acts, the efforts of the American government to bring pressure on other governments to take a strong stand against hijackers, and the pleas of pilots and the public, the problem seems as far from solution as it had been before.

However great the obstacles to space travel were to American technicians and planners, they seemed minor compared to travel on earth. Problems that defied solution were massive traffic tie-ups on streets and highways, deteriorating commuter and long-distance trains, congested airlanes between the major population centers, especially in the "Northeast Corridor" between Boston and Washington, and the attendant pollution from millions of private automobiles, municipal buses, aircraft, and ships and boats.

Rail travel was regarded by some as one means of alleviating the congestion of highways. Yet the outlook was poor. The nation's largest rail system, the Penn Central, filed for bankruptcy and had to be reorganized. It applied for Federal loan guarantees. A bill authorizing the Secretary of Transportation to guarantee loans up to $125 million was enacted. The government poured funds into a fast, efficient Metroliner between Washington and New York. Remedies for improving train service were the introduction of new equipment and fast service (like the Metroliner), relief from local property taxes for the railways, more labor cooperation aimed at eliminating practices like feather-bedding which increased costs and lent little to service, and more imaginative management that would make passenger rail service more attractive and efficient.

A whole new system of passenger railway service

(AMTRAK) went into effect in the spring of 1971 when the National Railroad Passenger Corporation, aided by a big grant from Congress, took control of all passenger service and reduced or cut service altogether in some states, including South Dakota and Wyoming. The Department of Transportation was given more power over railway safety. It was empowered by the Urban Mass Transportation Assistance Act (1970) to obligate over $3 billion over the next five years to help municipal bus and subway systems as the first segment of a $10 billion, twelve-year program.

Water transportation became another major concern of the nation. After eighteen years of construction by the U.S. Army Corps of Engineers, the President dedicated the vast Arkansas River project in June 1971. The elaborate system of locks and dams and other improvements made Tulsa, Oklahoma, a seaport connected to the Mississippi and to the Gulf of Mexico. Arkansas and Oklahoma now had access to the sea and coal, fertilizer, oil, wheat, iron, and steel, could move more easily to other American centers and to foreign ports. Further, the project was aimed at arresting devastating floods which used to paralyze the area and, as a bonus, at providing abundant electricity.

The Maritime Revitalizing Act of 1970 gave government aid in ship construction and in operating subsidies to bulk carriers. It freed the St. Lawrence Seaway from paying the annual interest on its fixed debt to head off an increase in rates to ships using the facility. The Merchant Marine Act of 1970, the first major revision of maritime law in over three decades, was an extensive effort to revitalize the U.S. merchant marine by seeking to build 30 ships per year for ten years with the long-range goal of increasing cargo capacity by three to four times. Government subsidies to shipbuilders would be progressively reduced. To help reduce costs the Maritime Administration adopted two standard ship designs that would cut down costs involved by using many designs and that would increase savings in operation.

GENERAL NOTES

Perhaps greater heed was given by many Americans to the weather or outbursts of nature, to sports, and television, than to foreign or domestic problems. Among the natural disasters were the earthquake in the Los Angeles area on February 9, 1971, and the series of tornadoes that cut through Louisiana, Mississippi, and Tennessee, about two weeks later, bringing casualties and destruction of property.

Ferment and protest touched amateur and professional sports. An increasing number of athletes no longer were concerned with building character or winning for the sake of the team and its sponsoring city. They wanted higher salaries and to promote their political and social goals. The National Football League players, for example, boycotted training camp until they received increases in pensions and benefits. Some college athletes protested the war in Southeast Asia, and some blacks spoke out against racial prejudices. Curt Flood, a highly paid black outfielder, was traded by the St. Louis Cardinals to the Philadelphia Phillies after the 1969 season, but refused to go. He sued organized baseball for over $3 million and brought suit to be allowed to play wherever he chose despite the so-called "reserve clause" that bound players to the team which originally signed them until they were sold or traded. Flood charged that he was a slave for a team against his will.

The Baltimore Orioles defeated the Cincinnati Reds in the 1970 World Series. In the following season, the World Series were taken by the Pittsburgh Pirates over the favorite Orioles. Professional football's Super Bowl championship for the 1970 season went to the Baltimore Colts over the Dallas Cowboys on January 17, 1971, but the following year the Cowboys beat the Miami Dolphins. The death in 1970 of the respected Ernie Lombardi, formerly of the Green Bay Packers and recently of the Washington Redskins, saddened sports fans. In boxing Joe Frazer defeated Jimmy Ellis for the heavyweight crown in February 1970, and successfully defended his title against Muhammed Ali (Cassius Clay), who had figured in the news repeatedly for his outspoken opinions and for the Supreme Court reversal in 1971 of his conviction on draft evasion.

In the most popular television show, *All in the Family,* the protagonist was a blue-collar "rightist" who favored law and order and President Nixon. His name, Archie Bunker, passed into the language as a thumbnail identification of the jingoistic, intolerant, blue-collar worker who opposed negroes, liberals, homosexuals, and welfare recipients. His adversaries in and out of his family prevailed over him every time, yet surprisingly Archie became something of a hero for "standing up for America."

There was a surfeit of sex in books as witness these 1970 best sellers: *The Sensuous Woman* by "J" *Everything You Wanted to Know About Sex* by David Reuben, and *Human Sexual Inadequacy* by William Masters and Virginia E. Johnson. Other widely read volumes were Joseph P. Lash's account of President and Mrs. Roosevelt, *Eleanor and Franklin,* and Charles A. Lindbergh's *Wartime Journals.* The yearning for the old fashioned "boy-meets-girl" theme probably explained the great popularity of *Love Story* by Erich Segal. Of more literary value was Eudora Welty's *Losing Battles.*

In the following year especially notable were George Garrett's *Death of the Fox* (an historical novel centering on Sir Walter Raleigh); Herman Wouk's *The Winds of War,* dealing with the U.S. experience in World War II; John Updike's *Rabbit Redux*, and *Flannery O'Connor: the Complete Stories,* a collection by a master stylist. There was no dearth of novels and books with political themes, including Philip Roth's attack on Nixon, *Our Gang,* on the war in Vietnam, and on youth (James A. Michener's *Kent State*).

Interest in religion was lively in 1970–1971, though not in the sense of attending church. The denominations that seemed to retain their appeal were fundamentalist and noncompromising in character, or emphasized the personal and emotional aspects of religion. Some said that there was a spiritual awakening manifest in the "Jesus People," in evangelical revivals, and in the pentecostal movement in Protestant and Catholic churches. Another trend was the decline in social activism espoused by the larger churches and congregations. Church-related social projects of some of the largest denominations had to be cut back in the face of the money squeeze. Conservative laymen contested liberal churchmen entrenched in national headquarters over the clerical militancy on civil rights, the war in Southeast Asia, fair housing, aid to the inner cities, and integration of the schools.

That the activists had political influence was shown when clergymen lobbying for the American Jewish Congress, the U.S. Catholic Conference, the National Council of Churches, and the United Methodist Church, pressured the House of Representatives to reject a proposed constitutional amendment to put prayers back in the public schools, a proposal which was supported by conservatives like the Reverend Billy Graham.

Sharp divisions reflecting the differences within the nation at large were common in the churches. In the Protestant churches, differences over dogma and especially over the activism of ministers in political questions led to many bitter disputes and the withholding of financial contributions by some laymen. In the Catholic Church, conservatives (who opposed the rapid pace of reform in the "updating" of the Church after the Second Vatican Council) were at odds with "progressives" who through their near-monopoly of the Catholic press agitated for more drastic reform and greater activism. The significant number of priests who quit the ministry, or sisters who abandoned their convents to be "relevant," weakened Catholic elementary and high schools. Other schools faced the bleak prospects of declining enrollments, reduced financial resources, and mounting costs, amid a widespread belief that many Catholic teachers had lost sight of religious and moral goals and were muddling through. The severest challenge to the Roman Catholic Church was the readiness of many theologians and teachers of religion to express opinions in doubtful conformity with traditional church teachings.

INDEX

Abortion legislation, 129
Agnew, Spiro T., 25; attacks news media, 15, 46
Air highjacking, 68, 132–34
Albert, Carl B., 19, 26
Alcatraz, occupation of by Indians, 111
Allende, Salvador, 50, 57
All in the Family, 137–38
Apollo moon flights, 130–31
Arab guerrillas, 67–68; air highjackings, 68, 132–33; and Jordan crisis, 68
Armed forces, drug abuse in, 22, 44; erosion of morale, 42–43. *See also* Vietnam War
Army Mathematics Research Center, University of Wisconsin, bombing of, 113
Arkansas River project, 135
Attica prison riot, 109–10
Automobiles, 71; excise tax repealed, 77; and pollution, 21, 134

Bangla Desh, created, 63–64; American supplies to, 64. *See also* Pakistan conflict
Berrigan, Reverend Philip, 11, 97
Blackmun, Harry A., 85
Black Panther Party, 9, 106–7; on Attica riot, 110; prison activity of, 108
Blacks, discontent with government, 9, 97, 98; economic status, 71, 97–98; influential positions held by, 99, 100; migration of, 100; militancy, 97, 105–8; new goals, 105; student incidents, 112; and Supreme Court decisions, 101–3. *See also* Integration; Racial discrimination
Boeing Aircraft Company, 76
Boggs, Hale, 26; accuses J. Edgar Hoover of wiretapping, 11
Bombing, criminal, 9, 117; of Army Mathematics Research Center, 113; of Capitol, 9; of Soviet Aerflot offices in New York, 58
Books, 46, 138
Brandt, Willy, 53, 54
Budget, Federal, 76; deficit spending, 76, 81
Burger, Warren E., on the judiciary, 84, 85
Busing issue, 101–5; and judiciary, 84, 103; public response to, 9, 103–4
Butz, Earl L., 18, 27

Cabinet, 17, 18
Calley, William L., Jr., 42–43
Cambodia, war in, 33–35; Congress opposes, 37; domestic and foreign reaction, 36; and student unrest, 33, 112
Canada, U.S. relations with, 21, 53, 78; Russian overtures toward, 57
Capitol (building), bomb in, 9
Carswell, George H., 85
CBS, and *Selling of the Pentagon,* 46
Census (1970), 69–70
Chiang Kai-shek, 41, 61
"Chicago Seven," 87; acquitted, 96
Chile, U.S. involvement in, 50; agreement with Russia, 57
China, Communist. *See* Peoples Republic of China
China, Nationalist. *See* Republic of China
Chisolm, Shirley, on blacks and party system, 100
Civil disobedience, 14
Civil Rights Movement, 97; failure of, 98–99, 105; new goals, 105
Clean Air Act, 21
Computerization of information, 10; and government "snooping," 10–11
Connally, John B., Cabinet appointment, 17
"Consciousness III," 116
Consumer affairs, 83
Congress, U.S., Black Caucus in, 101; composition of 91st, 19; of 92nd, 26; conservative coalition in, 32; and crime, 21–22, 23–24; defense spending, 28, 39, 46; economic measures, 80, 81; educational appropriations, 105, 119; girl pages in Senate, 126; legislative clashes with Nixon, 20, 27, 31–32; pollution measures, 21; and Supreme Court, 85–87; and taxes, 31; and 26th Amendment, 89; and war in Southeast Asia, 37, 38–39.
Cooper–Church Amendment, 39
Cost of Living Council, 77, 80
Commission on Human Rights, 98
Council of Economic Advisers, 77
Council on Environmental Quality, 21
Crime, 9, 10, 23–24
Cuba, air hijackings to, 132; relations with Russia, 57, 58

141

INDEX

Davis, Angela, trial of, 107–8
Defense, national, and B-52 controversy, 46; cut-back in programs, 75
Democratic Party, blacks and, 99, 100; gains in 1970 elections, 25; platform of, 25
Department of Justice, 21–22
Diem, Ngo Dinh, overthrow and assassination of, 95
District of Columbia Crime Bill, 21
Dollar, devaluation of, 53, 78, 79; inflated value of, 74; and world monetary crisis, 76, 78
Douglas, William O., investigation of, 85–86
Draft, 39, 89–90
Drug abuse, 22, 23; in armed forces, 22, 24; and youth culture, 118, 120

Earth Day, 21, 121
Economy, national, 70–83; government attempts to bolster, 75–78, 80–83; value of, 72; New Economic Program, 77–78; problems of 72–76
Egypt, and Middle East crisis, 67, 68; Russian arms and military presence in, 50, 67, 69
Ehrlichman, John, 17
Elections, of 1970, 25–26; success of blacks in, 100–101
Ellsberg, Daniel, and Pentagon Papers, 91
Emergency Employment Act, 7
England, plane hijacked by Arabs, 133; Tristar project with U.S., 28
Equal Employment Opportunities Commission, 124–25
Ervin, Sam J., on government "snooping," 10
Exports, decrease in, 80
Europe, demand for U.S. grain, 73; monetary revaluation in, 53; U.S. concern for defense of, 54; U.S. relations with, 50–51, 53; U.S. troops in, 51, 54

Farm groups, 74; oppose Butz nomination, 18; crop subsidies increased to, 81
Federal Commission on Obscenity, 12
Federal Reserve Board, 75, 76, 81
Flood, Curt, and baseball law suit, 136–37
Food, soaring price of, 73–74
Food stamps, 75
Ford, Gerald R., 19, 85
Foreign aid, reduction of, 48
Foreign policy, outlined 47–48. *See also* Middle East crisis; Vietnam War; and entries on countries
Friedan, Betty (*The Feminine Mystique*), 126
Fulbright, William, Laos proposal of, 34

Gandhi, Indira, 53; on Pakistan crisis, 65
Gold, and dollar crisis, 78, 79, 80
Grain, sale of to Russia, 55; increased demand abroad, 73–74
Greece, U.S. defense shipments to, 54
Gross National Product (GNP), 71, 72; and General Motors strike, 73

Haight–Ashbury, decline of, 118
Haldemann, H. R., 15, 17
Hardin, Clifford M., 18
"Harrisburg Seven," 97
Heath, David, meeting with Nixon, 53, 79
Hickel, Walter J., criticizes Nixon, 17
Hoffman, Julius J., and "Chicago Seven," 87, 96
Homosexuality, and "gay rights," 12; and women's movement, 129
"Honor America Day," 13
Hoover, J. Edgar, criticized, 11
Housing, 24
Hussein, Ali Ibn, King of Jordan, 68

Imports, U.S., ten percent surcharge on, 62, 77, 78; lifted, 54, 79
Income, average annual, 71; of non-whites, 97
India, and Pakistan conflict, 63–64; Russian alliance with, 64
Indians, American, 110–11
Inflation, 73–74, 76–77, 80; and grain sales to Russia, 55; and Vietnam War, 76
Insurance, hospitalization and life, 71
Integration, 98, 99, 104; abandoned as black goal, 105; *de facto* segregation in North, 98, 100; and Supreme Court, 101–3
Interest rates, and inflation, 75, 76
Israel, emigration of Soviet Jews to, 58; and Middle East crisis, 66–69; public opinion against, 66; U.S. planes to, 67, 68, 69

Jackson State College, Mississippi, 112–13
Japan, U.S. relations with, 61–63, 73; yen revalued, 79
Jarring, Dr. Gunnar, and Middle East, 67, 68
"Jesus People," 121, 138
Jewish Defense League (JDL), 58
Johnson, Lyndon B., actions of revealed in Pentagon Papers, 93–94; lets hair grow, 123; policies lead to inflation, 72, 74
Jordan, 67; guerilla crisis, 68

Kahane, Rabbi Meir, and JDL, 58
Kennedy, Edward M., 19; and Pakistan, 64

INDEX

Kent State University incident, 36, 112, 118; grand jury indictments, 113–14
Kissinger, Dr. Henry A., 51; plot to kidnap, 11, 97; visit to Peking, 59
Kosygin, P. Aleksei N., visits Canada, 57
Kudirka, Simas, attempted defection of, 56
Kunstler, William, 96, 109

Laos, invasion of, 34
"Law and order" advocates, 13, 96
Legislative Reorganization Act of 1970, 19
Lindsay, John V., antiwar sympathy, 36
Lockheed Aircraft Corporation, 28

McNamara, Robert, 91
Mansfield, Mike J., 19, 26, 51; on Nixon, 32; and Vietnam War, 38, 39
Marijuana, 22
Mariner 9, 131–32
Medina, Capt. Ernest, 42, 43
Merchant Marine Act of 1970, 135–36
Middle East crisis, growing tension of, 66–67; U.S. peace initiatives, 67, 68
Movies, "sexploitation' in, 11
Moynihan, Daniel P., 99
Mylai incident, 42–44; and moral of armed forces, 44, 45

Nader, Ralph, 84, 121–22
Nasser, Gamal Abdal, 68
National mood, 7–9, 12, 13–14; desire for isolationism, 49; war weariness, 49
Nerve gas, Defense Department disposal of challenged, 45
"New isolationism," 47, 48
New York City, "bomb factory" explosion in, 112; as 51st state, 29; "hard hat" demonstration in, 36–37, 119
New York Times, and Pentagon Papers, 90, 91
Nixon, Richard M., 9, 21, 23, 25, 49; China policy, 16, 58–61; and Cabinet, 17–18; Congressional victories, 27–28, 32; conservative opposition to, 15, 16–17; diplomatic journeys abroad, 51, 53; economic and fiscal policy, 27, 75–82; Indian policy, 110–11; legislative battles with Congress, 20, 27; Middle East policy, 66–68; nuclear warfare policy, 52–53; and the press, 15; and racial issues, 99, 104, 105, 110; Russian policy, 54–55; revenue-sharing programs, 29, 77; State of the Union address (1970), 19, 20; "State of the World" message, 52, 53, 54; Supreme Court nominations, 27, 85–87; Vietnam policy, 17, 25, 33; welfare program, 30–31
Nixon, Tricia, marriage of, 15

North Atlantic Treaty Organization (NATO), 56
North Vietnam, 41; involvement in Laos and Cambodia, 32, 33; and Pentagon Papers, 94; U.S. raids on, 41–42
Nuclear warfare, U.S. and world discussions on, 52–53, 55

Okinawa, returned to Japan, 62
"One man-one vote" ruling, 88

Pakistan conflict, 63–65; U.S. involvement in, 65–66
Paris peace talks, 32, 39
Penn Central Railroad, bankruptcy of, 73, 134
Pentagon Papers controversy, 90–96; and reexamination of Vietnam War, 93–96
Peoples Republic of China (Communist), and Pakistan, 65; seated in UN, 48, 61; U.S. relations with, 58–59, 61
"Phase Two," 80, 81
"Ping-pong diplomacy," 59
Pollution, 19, 20–21; and transportation, 134
Pompidou, Georges, meets with Nixon, 53, 79; JDL protests U.S. visit of, 58
Population, growth rate of, 69–70
Pornography, restrictions on lessened, 12
Postal Reorganization Act of 1970, 18; and sex-oriented advertising, 12
Powder Ridge rock festival, 119
Powell, Lewis F., Jr., 86
Press, 46, 59, 108; attacked by Agnew, 15; Catholic, 139; exposes Mylai incident, 42; freedom of, and Pentagon Papers, 93
Prisons, and prisoner rights, 108–9; riots in, 109–10
Protests and demonstrations, 35–37; by "hard hats," 36–37, 119; for Soviet Jews, 58; by veterans against Cambodian involvement, 38; for women's rights, 125–26, 127. *See also* Student unrest

Racial discrimination, 98; black athletes speak against, 136; in North, 98, 100
Radical activism, 9–10; of clergy, 11, 97, 138–39; of Indians, 111. *See also* Black Panthers; Student unrest
Rehnquist, William H., 86–87
Reich, Charles A. (*The Greening of America*), 116
Religion, 138–40; "Jesus People," 121, 138; Jewish Defense League, 58; radical clergy, 11, 97, 139; Roman Catholic Church, divisiveness within, 138–39; and women's movement, 127; and youth movement, 121
Republican Party, platform of, 25; and 1970 elections, 25–26

INDEX

Revenue-sharing, 29, 77
Republic of China (Nationalist), expulsion of from UN, 48, 61; U.S. relations with, 41, 61
Rockefeller, Nelson A., and Attica riot, 109–10
Rogers, William, 52; and Middle East, 67, 68, 69
Rusk, Dean, on U.S. motives in Vietnam, 94–95
Russia, 55, 58, 61, 132; clash of interests with U.S., 56, 66; Cuban relations, 57, 58; and Egypt, 50, 67, 69; growing prestige, 50, 65; Latin American relations, 56, 57; Middle East relations, 50, 57, 66–69; nuclear arms talks with U.S. 55; and Pakistan conflict, 65
Russo, Anthony, 91

Scranton Report, on student unrest, 113
"Science depression," 75, 132
Seale, Bobby, 96, 106, 107
Selling of the Pentagon (documentary), 46
Sex, in books, 138; in movies, 11; and youth culture, 119
Sihanouk, Prince Norodom, deposed, 34
Social Security benefits, increased, 31
Space program, 75, 130–32
Spain, defense agreement with U.S., 54
Spartan missile test, 47
Sports, 136–37
Strategic Arms Limitations Talks, 55
Strikes, 73; General Motors, 73; postal workers, 18
Student unrest, 38, 111–16; of blacks, 112; and Cambodia, 36, 112; decline, 118–19; legislative response to, 118. *See also* Kent State University incident; Youth culture
Suburbia, 24, 29, 70
Supersonic transport plane (SST), 28
Supreme Court, 12, 84; on blacks and integration, 101–3; decisions, 47, 85, 87–88, 125, 137; nominations, 27, 85–87; and Pentagon Papers, 91–92; and Vietnam War issues, 89–90, 91

Taxes, 31, 77
Television, 71; alleged liberal bias, 16;

criticizes military, 46; and student protest, 119; and women's movement, 125, 127
Transportation, 134–36
Trudeau, Pierre Elliott, 51, 57
26th Amendment, 89, 123

Unemployment, 9, 74–75; rate of, 74, 98
United Nations (UN), 48, 55; China controversy in, 41, 61; and Middle East, 67–68, 69; and Pakistan conflict, 65
University of California at Santa Barbara, 112
Urban crisis, 30

Veterans, 38, 45
Vietcong, 33, 34
Vietnam War, 32–33, 40–42; and Congress, 38–39; Mylai incident, 42–44; and Pentagon Papers, 93–96; and Supreme Court rulings, 89–90; troop withdrawals, 32, 38, 39, 41; Vietnamization, 33, 41
Voting age, lowered to eighteen, 24, 88–89; 26th Amendment, 89, 123

Wage-price controls, 75, 77–78; price "freeze," 78, 81
Wallace, George C., attacks busing, 104
Walsh, Bishop James, released by Chinese 59,
Washington Post, and Pentagon Papers, 90
Weathermen (radical group), 10
Welfare system, 30–31, 77; "welfare mess," 9, 30
West Germany, "Ostpolitik" policy of, 49; U.S. relations with, 49, 51, 53; and value of mark, 53, 78, 79
Wiretapping, questionable use of by Federal government, 11
Women's Liberation movement, 124–130; background, 124–25; goals and issues, 126–29; militant aspect, 125–26

Youth culture, analyzed, 116–23; disillusionment of, 117–18, 122; "establishment politics" of, 121–22

DATE DUE